D1712810

Tri-level Identity Crisis

Tri-level Identity Crisis

—— Children of First-Generation Immigrants ——

EDITED BY

Tapiwa N. Mucherera,
Chris Kiesling, AND
Anne Kiome Gatobu

PICKWICK *Publications* · Eugene, Oregon

TRI-LEVEL IDENTITY CRISIS
Children of First-Generation Immigrants

Pickwick Publications
An Imprint of Wipf and Stock Publishers
199 W. 8th Ave., Suite 3
Eugene, OR 97401

www.wipfandstock.com

PAPERBACK ISBN: 978-1-62564-552-4
HARDCOVER ISBN: 978-1-4982-8602-2
EBOOK ISBN: 978-1-7252-4924-0

Cataloguing-in-Publication data:

Names: Kiome Gatobu, Anne, editor. | Kiesling, Christopher, editor. | Mucherera, Tapiwa N., 1964–, editor.

Title: Tri-level identity crisis : children of first-generation immigrants / edited by Tapiwa N. Mucherera, Chris Kiesling, and Anne Kiome Gatobu

Description: Eugene, OR : Pickwick Publications, 2020 | Includes bibliographical references.

Identifiers: ISBN 978-1-62564-552-4 (paperback) | ISBN 978-1-4982-8602-2 (hardcover) | ISBN 978-1-7252-4924-0 (ebook)

Subjects: LCSH: United States—Emigration and immigration. | United States—Ethnic relations. | Americanization.

Classification: LC3731 .T74 2020 (print) | LC3731 .T74 (ebook)

Manufactured in the U.S.A.   07/30/20

Contents

Section III: Intervention Models

I

Tri-level Identity Crisis

1

Introduction

*General Identity Crisis and Its Implication
to Immigrants' Identity Development*

—CHRIS KIESLING, ANNE KIOME GATOBU,
AND TAPIWA N. MUCHERERA

THE MOMENT AN IMMIGRANT child (other than from Europe or born to Caucasian parents) steps on the North American soil, s/he is automatically considered a minority. A child of similar age who migrates from Europe, born of Caucasian parents, is automatically placed with the majority group. The current set up of the North American system is such that Caucasians (Whites) who are in power make the majority group, and those who come from places such as Africa, Asia, or Latin America—because of their birth place, accent or skin color—are readily categorized into the minority group. These immigrants do not fit the North American born minority model, because they are bringing with them some pre-determined cultural values that are usually in conflict with the North American values. The immigrant children, as any other minority in North America, have to deal with much racism and prejudice as inescapable as the air they breathe. Usually most new immigrants are oblivious to the racism and prejudices because it is not a default worldview from where they come. Soon enough they realize it is their new reality. They must contend with racism as they can neither escape their heritage nor the way the majority perceives them.

It does not matter what class these immigrant minorities belonged to in their country of origin, in North America they now acquire a new identity of being a minority. These children now have to deal with an identity development based on their status of being minorities in a majority culture.

A few months after landing in North American, minority children find that they are also on a collision course of cultural and moral values.

In the following discussion, we establish the general identity crisis of all adolescent children irrespective of geographical location or cultural context. This is followed by a brief discussion of the identity crisis of minority persons living in a majority culture. Immigrant children experience the general identity crisis as part of their developmental maturity. They also experience being a minority within majority culture that favors those of white privilege. But to compound this further, they are also navigating between values of their native country embedded in what their parents and grandparents hold sacred, and the value system embedded in Western cultural institutions. It is this compounding of forces in the matrix of American immigrants that we believe manifests in a unique experience of dissonance—a phenomenon that we have chosen to refer to as a *Tri-Level Identity Crisis*.

General Identity Crisis and Its Implication for Ethnic-Immigrant Identity Formation

Erik Erikson posited that the central psychosocial task presented to adolescents in the West is the formation of a consolidated ego identity. With good resolution of this identity, a young adult could enter the various domains of adult engagement (occupational, educational, familial, political, religious) with a secure sense of competence, meaning, and purpose. Erikson in fact, described identity as a secure sense of personal sameness and historical continuity, yielding the ability to transcend any particular moment or circumstance.[1] The necessity of identity consolidation he believed would be prompted naturally as young adults moved through various familial and societal engagements. If early childhood deficits or lack of social support during these years hampered identity formation; psychological, emotional, and social maladjustment could occur resulting in negative developmental outcomes. But what happens when historical continuity is disrupted? When an immigrant teenager experiences themselves differently in the presence of parents than with peers? And when movement between family and societal contexts makes any sense of identity consolidation seem elusive?

One of the most widely used conceptualizations for studying identity formation among adolescence in the West over the past fifty years has been

1. Erikson, *Childhood and Society; Identity.*

a model proposed by Jim Marcia.[2] Marcia suggested that the identity status of an individual could be measured based on two dimensions: (1) *exploration*—the presence or absence of a crisis indicated by the degree of an active period of deliberately considering and experimenting with alternatives; and (2) *commitment*—the presence or absence of movement toward ideological and interpersonal convictions. Marcia's design offers four quadrants or categories of identity status:

> *Diffused*—characterized by an absence of both exploration and commitment, a disabling of the capacities needed for identity formation

> *Foreclosed*—defined by commitment based on parental or societal imposition of values without a period of exploration

> *Moratorium*—indicative of involvement in active deliberation without yet having arrived at sustained commitments

> *Achieved*—determined by clear commitment that follows an active period of searching resulting in internalization and owning of commitments for oneself.[3]

A good body of research now exists that supports a progressive movement over time from diffusion or foreclosure toward identity achievement. Identity achievement and moratorium have shown significant correlation with adaptability, higher levels of moral reasoning, reflectivity in decision-making, satisfaction in relationships and capacity for cognitive complexity. By contrast, research shows that the foreclosed status correlates with difficulties in problem solving, lower self-esteem, high need for social approval, and rigidity in belief system. Further, identity diffusion shows outcomes more consistent with lower levels of moral reasoning, avoidance of coping with problems, and higher levels of compulsivity.[4]

The importance of this research for immigrant populations living in the West is three-fold. It gives description to the normative ego developmental process for all teenagers—what we regard as first level identity crisis. It also provides theoretical conceptualization for processes through which minority culture youth fashion an identity amidst majority culture—what we regard as second level identity crisis, and it offers key insight into the

---

2. Marcia, "Development and Validation"; "Identity in Adolescence."

3. Marcia, "Development and Validation"; "Identity in Adolescence."

4. St. Louis and Liem, "Ego Identity."

development of ethnic identity formation distinct to immigrants—what we regard as third level identity crisis. Ethnic minority individuals progress from a state of unexamined ethnicity (diffusion or foreclosure) through a period of exploration into the meaning and implications of their group membership (moratorium), moving finally to an achieved ethnic identity characterized by the development of a secure sense of oneself as a member of an ethnic group.[5] For the ethnic minority teenager in the US the question "who am I?" inevitably includes aspects of race, color and history associated with one's ancestry. By ethnic identity we are here referring to "one's sense of belonging to an ethnic group in the part of one's thinking, perceptions, feelings and behavior that is due to ethnic group membership."[6] Hence for minority youth, questions of identity carry the rider, "Who am I as an African American?"; "Asian American?"; "Native American?"; etc.

Navigating the waters of ethnic identity formation can be especially turbulent for immigrant children from more traditional cultures. The clash between Western individualism and collective, communal expectations create conflicting sets of identification models, role expectations, and socio-cultural norms that leave diaspora teens and young adults especially susceptible to identity problems.[7] The developmental task communicated to children and teens in Western culture is to develop mastery over one's environment and move progressively toward greater autonomy and self-reliance. The hallmark of this development is typically a process of increased separation from parents and family toward achieving a sense of individuality and differentiation. This is usually accompanied by such things as experimentation with changing vocational aspirations; encouragement to socialize with new peer groups; becoming financially independent; involvement in romantic relationships; and making one's own decisions about religious involvement and political orientation. Hence, adolescence and emerging adulthood in the West often requires a renegotiation of one's connectedness to the family, with both the young adult and the parents accommodating to the expectation that the process of deciding who a young adult will be or become is now increasingly in the domain of the individual.[8]

In more collectivist cultures, identity may largely already be defined by role expectations that exist within a more extended familial and cultural

5. Phinney, "Stages of Ethnic Identity Development"; "Three Stage Model."

6. Rotheram and Phinney, "Introduction."

7. Kundu and Adams, "Identity Formation, Individuality, and Connectedness."

8. Kundu and Adams, "Identity Formation, Individuality, and Connectedness."

community. In these cultures, the shift from childhood to adulthood (note the absence of adolescence as a recognized distinct stage of the life) may not be concerned with separation from family for the sake of increased individuation. Instead, development assumes the acceptance of greater responsibility for one's place within the family or clan itself.[9] Rather than the emphasis being placed on autonomous choice to self-define one's place in society, the journey to adulthood in traditional society entails the attempt of elders and peers to clarify the many roles one is expected to occupy and the responsibilities that accompany those roles. Hence, ethnic identity may be experienced as something more ascribed than chosen.[10]

In the West, morals and values have been ensconced in a body of written law, giving definition to what is acceptable and what is punishable behavior. Authority figures are given power to enforce laws in such a way that punishments and consequences provide the means for directing behavior and relationships between citizens. Laws do not have to elicit any emotion or feeling to be binding, they simply have to be observed. As long as one is not breaking the law, he or she is regarded as a good, law-abiding citizen and can harmoniously live in regular society.

For most non-Western cultures however, morals and values are communally transacted. They are meant to become obligatory and determine normative behavior not as a matter of law but as a matter of the heart mediated through relationships. For instance, respecting one's parents is one of the highest shared moral standards in the non-western world, but rarely is it ensconced in law. Its manifestation differs with varying communities but can generally be seen in *how* one speaks to his or her parents or how one relates to his/her parents and other seniors with respect [in itself a term that has differing meanings]. Speaking back, arguing or saying any ill to one's parents is an ultimate moral failure and dishonors the whole family. In some societies it might even be regarded as bringing to the family a curse from God and ancestors. Even if the parents are wrong about something, the child is expected to find the humblest way to bring this to their attention but not blurt it out as though in competition or disgrace to the parent. The phrase "*children are to be seen not to be heard*" is a good example of an expectation that stems from this example of a moral-guiding, communal ethic rather than a legal-guiding society. The conflicting way that morals and values are shaped and held by a society creates dissonance between children and first

9. Ahmed, "Adolescent Development."

10. Côté and Levine, *Identity Formation, Agency, and Culture.*

immigrant parents, an experience of third-level identity crisis that will inevitably show up in many of the chapters of this book.

Anne recalls a heated conversation that ensued in her household with one of her sons who was seeking to go to a sleepover at a friend's house. Recognizing how difficult it was for him to secure parental permission to stay at a house with someone his parents had never met, and contrasting this with friends who got easy permission with a simple phone call home, he commented in exasperation "I wish I were normal." Anne recognized that the sleepover had totalized the experience of her child feeling essentially different. In this instance, a classic example of a clash in the movement to identity formation is seen. When the western child asked to stay at a friend for a sleepover, the parents recognized a need for the child to engage in self-differentiation towards identity. The immigrant parent on the other hand faces a complex rationale to reckon with: can I trust that my child will be safe in a home of people who represent those that do not trust me on the basis of my nationality? Can the immigrant parent trust that their child will be treated well by people she has never met in this racially divided world and/or society of the USA? When will this child grow to the maturity of appreciating closeness with family that does not choose friends over family? Why is a "sleepover" not part of our culture of visiting, that' is, the parents visit each other first before the sleepover? In this illustration then one can clearly see that the rationale used by either parent to make decisions about a sleepover is quite different. While the western parent recognizes this is a good maturational gesture towards independence and identity formation, the immigrant parent approaches it with caution and negative implications. Meanwhile, for the immigrant teenager, "Who am I?" expands into the form, "What do I really believe and how do I communicate that to my parents whose expectations of me are opposite from my peer's parents, and yet do so without sounding disrespectful?"

Seeking an amicable compromise between peers and parents for many immigrant children poses the challenge of living in bifurcated worlds. In most cases, the journey entails arguments, denouncements, warnings and consequences often accompanied by the pain of depression, loneliness, feeling different, and even self-hatred. Rapprochement with parents often feels like resignation to never be understood. Immigrant parents regard as disobedience and disrespect any attempt by their child at asserting Western individuality by speaking his/her mind and arguing that a behavior is not illegal. Like Western children, conflict with parents sometimes leads to hidden behavior. However, whereas children raised in the West may find some vindication if the behavior is not technically illegal; immigrant children often carry deep guilt and shame as their conscience senses a moral breach and disaffiliation with the larger family and community. Consequently, immigrant parents may begin to feel dissonance and a fluctuating confidence as they question their own parenting style. Fear of the unknown fosters disillusionment and despair.

Indeed, the developmental outcomes targeted by divergent cultures may function to affect differing practices and norms across the lifecycle. Cultures emphasizing individuation may feel compelled to wean a child from the breast earlier, place an infant more quickly into separate sleeping quarters, take advantage of institutionalized care that provides opportunity for both parents to work, get a child toilet-trained earlier, and use less authoritarian means of discipline. Other differences may appear later in the life course. Cultures emphasizing traditional or collectivist norms may set stricter curfews, demand obedience from teenagers, restrict social activities and monitor romantic allurements, look for family/tribal compatibility in the seeking of a spouse, expect kin-keeping from their grown children, and sanction elders to become the carriers of tradition to younger generations. The identity crisis created in immigrant children will no doubt vary from teen to teen dependent on such things as: parental assimilation to American culture, adherence to spiritual faith, sibling order, geographic location in the United States, age of the child's exposure to the western world, family proximity and level of interaction with non-western families, and the level of parental cultural identity and sense of self.

Immigrant parents who have come from traditional cultures unaccustomed to recognizing adolescence or emerging adulthood as distinct stages of life carrying their own developmental tasks of increased individuation and autonomy may feel ill equipped to facilitate the resolution of conflict created by the clashes of culture during these years. To promote the preservation of their traditional culture that gave their own life anchoring and meaning, immigrant parents often attempt to promote traditional values and practices. After all, they reason that, that is how they were raised and they turned out well! Quite unwittingly, the host culture in this protective process can become demonized—e.g., "that corrupted American society."[11] Whereas there may be legitimacy to such cultural critiques, such brandishing creates a difficult double-bind for teenagers being raised in these

11. Kundu and Adams, "Identity Formation, Individuality, and Connectedness."

families. To succumb to decadent American values can be regarded as a damnable defiance of one's parents and heritage, as well as a denial of one's very ontology; but to not assimilate to the host culture is to suffer feelings of isolation, abnormality, or other consequences of disaffiliation.

Ethnic identity that is more salient in traditional culture has strong components of social development that tap deeply into feelings of belongingness. Hence, ethnic exploration typically involves the process by which individuals explore, learn, and become involved with their ethnic group. By contrast, ego identity that is so cherished in Western culture operates at the individual, and psychological level. Processes of individuation or differentiation are often pitted against aspects of connectedness, belonging or integration across many domains of identity.[12] In very traditional cultures, for example, a woman is not regarded as a person in her own right; rather her identity is defined by her parents when she is young, and when she becomes an adult her husband and his family redefine her identity.[13] More moderate examples might be the young man who works two jobs while attending college in order to financially support siblings back home or the young woman who ends a courtship on the basis of parental disapproval. Each of these may find their Western counterparts encouraging them to relinquish such filial piety and "live their own life." Indeed, in psychotherapy, such dispositions of connectedness to one family of origin may be misdiagnosed as diffused relationships or dependent disorders.

Research has begun to explore how parents from traditional cultures navigate these complicated waters with their young and some helpful conceptualizations are beginning to emerge. Strategies that "prepare the young for bias" such as teaching them how to respond to discrimination or subversive value judgments may prove to be more pro-social than strategies that "promote mistrust" such as inciting fear about the potential negative consequences of interacting with others. Family conversations that center discussion on values such as equality and coexistence may facilitate higher reasoning that equips the young best for adult interaction.[14]

12. Kundu and Adams, "Identity Formation, Individuality, and Connectedness."
13. Kundu and Adams, "Identity Formation, Individuality, and Connectedness."
14. Phinney, "Stages of Ethnic Identity Development."

A Particular Model of Racial Identity Development (for All Minorities)

In the following section we address some of the minority cultural identity crisis and development minority children have to face with special focus on the North American context, looking through the lens of Sue and Sue's "Racial/Cultural Identity Development Model" (R/CID Model). The model has five stages of identity development: Conformity, Dissonance, Resistance and Immersion, Introspection, and Integrative.

Sue and Sue characterize this first stage, *conformity*, by noting the eagerness to "fit in" that most minorities who leave their country of origin and migrate to North America feel despite bringing with them their own culture.[15] Much energy may be spent on trying to assimilate into the North American (White) culture at the expense of his/her own. Interestingly, the idea of trying to "fit in" is similar to what Sue and Sue say typifies even those minorities who are born into the North America experience:

> Similar to individuals in the pre-encounter stage . . . minority individuals are distinguished by their unequivocal preference for dominant cultural values over their own. White Americans in the United States represent their reference group, and the identification set is quite strong. Lifestyles, value systems, and cultural/physical characteristics that resemble White society are highly valued, whereas those most like their own minority group are viewed with disdain or may hold low salience to the person.[16]

As this stage is correctly named, the minority individual is aiming at developing an identity that suits the North American White cultural context. *Conformity* represents an absence of identity exploration. When first encountering a new culture, individuals may show no interest in actively searching for the meaning and importance of their ethnicity in their day-to-day functioning. They may uncritically adopt the values, preferences and attitudes of the majority culture, sometimes internalizing negative stereotypes of their own ethnic group held by those in the dominant society.[17]

The downside is that the environment is not as accommodating and nurturing of that new identity. Geographic distance and a lack of common interests tend to eliminate the likelihood of extended family from the

15. Sue and Sue, *Counseling the Culturally Diverse*, 297

16. Sue and Sue, *Counseling the Culturally Diverse*, 296.

17. Phinney, "Stages of Ethnic Identity Development," 34–35.

homeland becoming natural role models for immigrant children. Parents may attempt to bridge the chasm by encouraging phone calls, showing pictures of extended kin, and storytelling, but all too often immigrant teens fall under the influence of Western sports heroes, pop culture, or political icons. Consequently, ethnic minority youth growing up in diaspora movements may be at risk of failing to achieve a secure ego identity if they simply adopt attributes imputed to them by the dominant culture. Students in this state of unexamined ethnic identity often report the poorest self-concepts.

The fact that the minority is trying to fit into a context that is not accepting creates much tension in trying to assimilate. This subjective tension propels one into a posture of what Sue and Sue term as *dissonance*. How can one accept him/herself as a valued and respected individual member of the society, yet have to deal with the fact of trying to fit into a cultural value system that devalues him or her, feels oppressive, and sees one as inferior and inadequate? To fit into this oppressive cultural mold, the immigrant may first deny him/herself and look up to the White cultural values and system as superior. Seeing majority culture as one to be admired and emulated, they may internalize a sense of themselves as inferior and less intelligent. Sue and Sue say about the dissonance stage:

> No matter how much one attempts to deny his or her own racial/
> cultural heritage, an individual will encounter information or
> experiences that are inconsistent with culturally held beliefs, at-
> titudes, and values. An Asian American who believes that Asians
> are inhibited, passive, inarticulate, and poor in people relation-
> ships may encounter an Asian Leader who seems to break all
> these stereotypes. . . . A Latino/a who feels ashamed of his or
> her cultural upbringing may encounter another Latino/a who
> seems proud of his cultural heritage. An African American who
> believes that race problems are due to laziness, untrustworthi-
> ness, or personal inadequacies of his or her own group may
> suddenly encounter racism at a personal level. Denial begins to
> breakdown, which leads to a questioning and challenging of the
> attitudes/beliefs of the conformity stage.[18]

A shift begins to occur when the person in dissonance realizes that there is something problematic about the system, not about who s/he is as an individual or about his or her cultural group. S/he becomes aware that s/he has bought into false stereotypes about minorities. The person

---

18. Sue and Sue, *Counseling the Culturally Diverse*, 299.

begins to realize the numerous ways that ethnic identification and exploration is commonly more proximal and more salient for ethnic minority than for members of the majority group. The person starts to observe minorities who have tried to work hard to change their situation, yet the cultural system does not allow them to go past certain levels despite their efforts. In addition, these individuals become aware of the "glass ceiling" that minorities have to deal with in corporate America and in the "White world." This experience of being subjugated, insists that integration of ethnic identity becomes a part of ego development if it is to allow for the development of a positive self-concept.[19]

This realization about how society is set up impels the minority individual into the next stage of *resistance*. The resistance is against the oppressive White social systems and most of the times not necessarily against White individuals. Sue and Sue say the following about the resistance and immersion stage:

> The minority person tends to endorse the minority-held views completely and to reject the dominant values of society and culture. The person seems dedicated to reacting against White society and rejects White social, cultural and institutional standards as having no personal validity. Desire to eliminate oppression of the individual's minority group becomes an important motivation of individual's behavior. . . . There are considerable feelings of guilt and shame that in the past the minority individual has sold out his or her own racial and cultural group. . . . Anger is directed outwardly in a very strong way toward oppression and racism.[20]

In the resistance stage the minority realizes he has been sold a "bill of goods" and that what s/he has been taught about minorities in general (he or she included) is not true especially as it pertains to the stereotypes. The focus and energy at this stage is more on the dismantling of the unjust system rather than individual prejudices. The person in this stage realizes that there is power in numbers and so joins other minorities of like minds who are willing to work against injustice and inequality in any form. A reference group that validates a sense of self and provides a place of belonging may become increasingly critical during the adolescent and young adult years. Some individuals in the resistance stage may express anger, sourced in part in the sense of having sold out especially in the *conformity* stage. How could

---

19. Phinney, "Stages of Ethnic Identity Development," 34–49.

20. Sue and Sue, *Counseling the Culturally Diverse*, 301.

they have been so blind to buy into or want to join such a system that is so oppressive to one? The anger is both at the self and those who have created such a system. Individuals in this stage rely on their minority group for support yet the energy that drives them in that group is based on anger, even though it is anger at the system. As much as the anger is against an unjust and unequal system, this can be very draining for someone to fight a system that has been in place for over 400 years.

The next question then is; for these individuals to survive in such a system, how can they spend energy fighting to transform the system and yet be able to make an everyday living? In addition, some individuals also find themselves in situations where they feel they can work in changing the system yet have friends who are White, without experiencing any guilt feelings about those relationships. However, to please one's own group, and having a relationship with Whites may appear as "selling out." In other words, the minority group starts questioning how someone who is committed to change is able to "sleep with the enemy," so to speak. This is the *introspection* stage, of which Sue and Sue say:

> The individual begins to discover that this level of intensity of feelings (anger directed toward White society) is psychologically draining and does not permit one to really devote more crucial energies to understanding oneself or one's own racial-cultural group. . . . Often, in order to please the group (own group), the individual is asked to submerge individual autonomy and individual thought in favor of group good. A Latino/a individual who may form a deep relationship with a White person may experience considerable pressure from his or her culturally similar peers to break off the relationship because that White person is the "enemy." However, the personal experiences of the individual may, in fact, support this group view.[21]

In the introspection stage the individual has to balance the sense of the need for justice and yet maintain being in relationship with those who may look like the ones perpetuating the unjust system. One realizes that as much as Whites benefit from the racist system in place, not all Whites are supportive of the system. These minorities have to learn to bridge between the two worlds. They have to start learning to negotiate between two differing cultures that hold conflicting values. To feel grounded again, one has to go to the "internal self," to get a sense of who s/he is in such a

21. Sue and Sue, *Counseling the Culturally Diverse*, 302–3.

conflicting world. Hence the stage calls for *introspection*—accessing one's internal world and examining one's own mental and/or emotional state. In the introspection stage the individual is trying to resolve some of the dissonance created by the reality of a racist and unjust system; and the fact that they have friends and have been in relationship with some kind and justice-loving White people.

The process of introspection moves one to the next level of the *integrative awareness* stage, the balancing of a sense of the inner-self and security in light of an unjust society one has to exist. Sue and Sue say about the stage:

> Minority persons in this stage have developed an inner sense of security and now can own and appreciate unique aspects of their culture as well as those in US culture. Minority culture is not necessarily in conflict with White dominant cultural ways. Conflicts and discomforts experienced in the previous stage become resolved, allowing greater individual control and flexibility. There is now belief that there is acceptable and unacceptable aspects in all cultures and that it is very important for the person to be able to examine and to accept and reject those aspects of a culture that are not seen as desirable. . . . The minority person has a strong commitment to eliminate all forms of oppression.[22]

One of the key issues at this stage is that the minority person is not just focused on injustice to his/her own group, but is concerned about all forms of injustice. The individual is able to accept his/her own minority cultural values and aspects of the White cultural values without necessarily experiencing conflict. There is the realization that all cultures have aspects that are undesirable.

When the active exploration of these meanings leads to the acquisition of a clear, internalized, and confident sense of one's own ethnicity, identity achievement is said to have occurred. Preliminary studies show that young adult students who have integrated ethnic identity into an achieved ego identity report more positive psychosocial competencies that predict favorable outcomes in occupational, educational, political, and religious domains.[23] An immigrant child, or a child born to immigrant parents may wrestle with these issues of identity development at two conflicted levels. At one level, they have to live at home with parents who may be pushing the child to assimilate, while the same child is facing a racist environment

---

22. Sue and Sue, *Counseling the Culturally Diverse*, 304
23. St. Louis and Liem, *Ego Identity.*

in school, work, etc. How does one assimilate in a racist system? The child is caught in between the dilemma of respecting the parents' views over against standing up to an unjust system.

In the next chapters, we provide a more personal look into the life of immigrant families in the USA. This chapter then segues to the middle section of this book where we have assembled a group of scholars, asked them to conduct interviews and do research on those in their ethnic group who have immigrated to North America. Where possible we have asked each writer to: describe main avenues of migration to the United States, explore religious values and cultural traditions specific to their group, analyze unique challenges the group experienced in navigating Western culture (e.g., language, barriers, symbolism, immigration papers, stereo-types), and provide a window into the effects such challenges have had on their general life in the United States (financial, marital, familial, com-munication with children, community relationships, etc.). Through this examination we have tried to surface unique identity challenges from the family and society that contribute to an understanding of the multi-layered ways that immigrants establish an identity in America.

It is important that we offer a distinction made so well by Agwu Chi-naka[24] regarding first generation, 1.5 generation and second generation children. First generation immigrants are those who migrated to North America once they were already formed in their country of origin iden-tity. Usually those who migrate at college age and above will fall under this definition. According to Rumbaut and Ima, the 1.5 generation immigrants refer to those who immigrated to North America after school age.[25] The implication here is that they already have some social cultural influence of their country of origin in their formative years—an aspect that plays a major role when they experience tri-level identity crisis for better adjustment. The most known group is the second-generation immigrants who are mainly children of first generation immigrants born in North America. Though pre-school children born outside of north American may technically be termed as second-generation immigrants because of lack of influence of their cultural heritage, the reality of their immigration status has huge im-pact on their identity formation, especially towards their sophomore high school year as they begin to think of college opportunities. Those born in the US have access to whatever college they choose and do not have to

24. Agwu, *Acculturation and Racial Identity Attitudes*.

25. Strama, *Deconstructing the American Dream*.

think of immigration status or educational finances. They can easily get college loans through FAFSA. Those who came as children must now contend with these major differences and in some cases issues of deportation. While these might look like harmless differences, the ramifications are huge with regard to their still forming cultural and social identity. Such differences will sometimes be the reason that parents will be more cautious about allowing their young adults to enjoy all aspects of college, as they are afraid that the child may do things that are illegal and end up having their papers denied or deported. The highly politicized case of DACA children is a classic example of implications on identity formation of the two distinctive second generation immigrants. Generally, the chapters in this volume focus on first generation immigrant parents and their second generation children. However, we did not restrict authors to stay within these parameters, but allowed them to utilize categories that best helped them characterize the populations about which they are writing.

The last section of the book offers insightful ways of navigating and minimizing adverse dissonance in children of immigrants through communal-based rites of passages and through the adaptation of family palavers that we believe offer promise for smoother pathways as immigrant families navigate the perilous terrain of tri-level identity crises.

2 _____

Experiences of Immigrant Families in the West, with Special Reference to the USA

—ANNE KIOME GATOBU

IN ORDER TO UNDERSTAND the *third level identity crisis* of children of first generation immigrants, it is important to have some base knowledge of both their experience in the social realm and at home, as well as that of their parents. This chapter's objective is to help the reader get into the world of these families from both the perspective of the first generation immigrant parents and that of their children. It is therefore divided into two parts for ease of discussion, first to discuss the journey of parents navigating a new culture and second how such navigation translates into their parenting roles and the response of their children.

Parents Navigating a Foreign Culture

Ultimate Cultural Shock—Loss of Status

Speak to any immigrant person and they will each have an experience of some sort regarding cultural shock. For many, it is the seasonal changes and ensuing extreme weather changes (especially if coming from equatorial climates where the days are generally the same throughout the year). For these immigrants, the changes of four drastically different seasons are a phenomenon to which one never really gets used. The idea of snow and chilling icy cold is not one to which these immigrants really acclimate. Yet for others, cultural shock is experienced in the foreign foods they have to get used to, and the reality that familiar foods often found in specialty stores are five times as expensive in the US as they are in their home country. For instance, even after living in the US for seventeen years, I still have trouble buying a mango for $1.49 when I remember that fifty cents could buy a fifty-pound sack full of mangoes in Kenya! The same case applies to kale and collard greens. Greens, in Kenya acquired a popular name "*sukuma wiki*" which means "stretching the week" because of its availability in abundance and therefore cheapness—indeed a week stretcher for families with meager financial means. One can imagine the shock it elicits with the conversion of its cost of about $1.29 in the US to the Kenyan shilling. Other immigrants, experience cultural shocks in the form of language differences. One may have come from a country where English is an official school language and therefore believed themselves to have the command of the language—only to land in the US and realize they have a deep accent that most people complain about and sometimes one is relegated to not knowing English. This realization comes with an undercutting of one's confidence in communication in public especially among proficient English speakers. While these and other experiences are unique to geographical location and social context, as well as the experience of the immigrant, the one most cited by people as the greatest and most shocking is the loss of social status. This is especially pertinent to the experience of immigrants from Africa and Asia whose main reason for immigrating to the US is pursuit for higher education. Consider the following scenario for a moment which may give insight into what constitutes loss of social status: Most immigrants in pursuit of educational opportunities are generally the cream of their society in their home country either by virtue of higher education level which earned them recognition by a Western institution, or by virtue of coming from families with financial means. Many such immigrants also happen to be second career persons who have already been serving in recognized institutions and positions in their home country. They have been living in decent homes, and their kids have been attending private schools, which are affordable to the middle-class since public education is usually not desirable. Most of these people are regarded as dignified leaders in their communities. In most cases, they have live-in servants who cater to all the household needs, not necessarily because they are very rich but because it is the norm: servants are affordable and provide a necessary security against burglary. Some, especially married men, do not launder or iron their own clothes, or cook their own meals, or wash dishes.

Yet, because of the popular exposure to the West as a land of opportunity and the general mindset of the West as more developed and a first world country, the prospect of living and making an even better life in the first world captures their excitement. That is, until they arrive. In a couple of weeks reality sets in. One pastor whose experience was the typical immigrant loss of status shock captured the experience in these words:

> "At home I was respected, catered to by everyone around me, rubbed shoulders with heads of the state as their pastor, and in one month in the US I became a poor beggar who relied on the wishes of my sponsors. My children could not understand why they had to share a bedroom in our two-room school apartment when at our home in Africa they each had a huge room with en-suite bathroom."

The loss of status is not only associated with loss of material resources but also, and maybe more detrimental, the loss of a place of honor in the society and its ensuing impact on the ego and sense of self. The community leader who had an administrative assistant and hundreds of workers under his supervision, now becomes a student who according to immigration requirements can only work in the educational institution that sponsors his Visa. Unfortunately, the educational institution, because of limited work-study positions and institutionalized prejudice, only has the lowest of jobs open to international students. So the corporate manager or esteemed pastor in his country now finds himself/herself a cook in the school kitchen, or a custodian to clean toilets. Except for the few who come on a full scholarship (usually one international student per year or in some institution every two to four years), all international students somehow have to take the "lowest" paying job within the institution to survive! Men from these communities have the hardest time transitioning to these statuses because of the high esteem with which they are held back in their countries of origin. Women make the transition easier because of their greater resiliency and coping resources, developed from years of demand for their versatility and gender discrimination in their own countries.

Gender Roles Adjustments

Many men will therefore try to hold onto their status at least in the home where they can still wield some power. In many situations, this also becomes a battlefield with wives who, now without help of house servants, are overwhelmed and demand the fair share of responsibilities from their husbands. If the man was raised very traditionally with regard to gender expectations, the very necessity to be involved in the daily affairs of the home as cooking, cleaning, or changing diapers becomes yet another blow to his manhood. The impact of loss of status ripples through the whole family system: greater conflict between spouses leads to emotional withdrawal and depression, making them emotionally unavailable to each other at a time when they really need each other because of lack of meaningful community. The less supportive of each other they become, the less emotionally available they are to the nurture of their children. The more their status is eroded both at home and in society, the less confident they feel, and the more they mirror insecurity to their children.

It does not help the situation when generally the American society favors the woman of color over their men because of the stereotypical association of crime and violence with men of color. Often this translates to greater opportunities for the immigrant wife rather than her husband in terms of finding jobs, scholarships or promotions—yet another blow to the status for the man!

Challenges of Immigration Status

The passage to the US in recent years for most first generation immigrants is gained either in pursuit of education, through the green-card lottery, via an application for an HB-1 work visa for skilled profession labor, or through illegal immigration via the borders. Visas have their own specific requirements and time limits to maintain one's legal status. Hence, each passage poses its own set of challenges to the individual and family in general. For instance, those families that come on student Visa, usually have the F-1 or the J-1 visa. The spouse would then have a F-2 or J-2 Visa and is not allowed to work at all under the under this visa status, while the spouse with an F-1 Visa can only work the lowest paying jobs in their educational institution. In a country where life is generally expensive, this means the family must live below poverty level with very few forms of social help. Even when help is available, most immigrants are not aware of these resources. Some, even though aware, choose not to access it because of shame associated with coming from a place where they could adequately provide for their family.

The J-2 Visa has more leeway in terms of accessing work but even then, the holders experience a blow to their sense of self because the skills which may have been well respected in their countries are not recognized when they migrate. I am reminded a friend who was a well-accomplished dentist in Kenya, owning his own dental clinic and a staff of nine. In his country he was renowned, generally referred to as *"Daktari"* (Doctor)—one of the highest titles in the community. He had just lost his wife and wanted to give his children a new start by migrating to the United States. He followed all the proper channels thinking that when he got here he could easily get a job with his almost twenty years of dental experience. His first big shock was to discover that his whole training and experience was equivalent to zero years in the US. To even qualify to work as a dental hygienist or assistant he would have to go back to school. He bit the bullet and started a journey of seven years in dental school. The irony is that during his residency, the instructors usually looked up to him for insights and advice when faced with challenging dental work. Today, he owns three clinics in the U.S.A.—an accomplishment that required a long, humiliating journey. On the same vein, I met a lady who migrated after marrying her spouse who was already living in the US. In her country of origin, she had risen to a managerial position in one of the largest banks in her native country. When she migrated she expected to easily get back into her banking line since she had an undergraduate and a Master of Arts degree in banking and economics, only to realize that her degrees meant nothing in the USA. She could not even get a job as a teller in a bank because she was told she was over-qualified.

There is the also the plight of those who have no legal status because their Visa had expired or because they came without more permanent papers. Their challenge is even worse because they have to take jobs that are paid under the table and below minimum wage to support their families. They are constantly in hiding and must strictly instruct their children on how to avoid the law. The children are aware of their precarious position but must wrestle with the existential questions of "why them?" The children find themselves in constant dissonance about themselves and their families, noting the differences in social and economic status of families that surround them. The school system allows their children to be enrolled—but only through high school. After high school, no college will enroll their children. I am reminded of a family in a small town in Central Nebraska whose parents were some of the sweetest, most abiding citizens I knew. The small community loved them because they were helpful and polite. They had lived in this community for a long time but always took care not to get too close to anyone for fear that they might discover that they did not have papers. The wife always expressed how much she would have loved to go to the community college close by but could not. When the son, one of the most obedient and smart kids in the school, turned sixteen, I asked naively if he was excited that he could now drive. His mother was in tears and said he cannot get a driver's license. I understood exactly what she meant. The son lived through being taunted for not driving by his fellow classmate who could not be told the truth. Then when he completed high school, he had to face the fact that he could not enroll in college like his friends. How can anyone say young people are on the same playing ground and should just apply themselves? There are tons of stories of varied life experiences that tell us status matters in the mental, spiritual and economic welfare of first generation immigrant children.

Response to Prejudice

For most immigrants to the United States color and race have never been an issue. In fact, most report that they were not aware of their racial color until they had to fill out the immigration entry form at their point of entry. I remember not filling anything in on that field of the form because I had never described myself or even known that people are classified by color!

In cultural identity literature, this phenomenon has been well articulated by T. L. Cross[1] in the minority cultural development model. Unlike the normal minority cultural development that begins for minority Americans at a very early age, when they begin to ask the question of "who am I?" in a multicultural world, the immigrant does not begin this process until they have come to the US and are socially defined as a minority person of color. The obvious response of the immigrant is to attempt to conform to the majority culture—a natural remnant of identity in colonialism where the European is always considered superior due to technological and industrial advancement.

In time, this response changes as the raw experiences of racism and prejudice begin to encroach on the immigrant. For some who remain in this *conformity* stage to fit in and gain the benefits of conforming to the majority culture, there is a sense of repressing their needs and expressions. There is a sense of almost living an *imposter's life* foreign to who they truly

---

1. Cross, *Negro to Black Conversion Experience*, 13–17.

are. Enduring, false humility and amicability with the majority world, while allowing their real selves to emerge only in the familiarity of their fellow ethnic friends and family, characterize such a life. One may call it a "double-life" to distinguish it from the pathological label of bi-polarism. For others who manage to move through the stages of cultural identity development to the *Integrative Awareness* stage, the journey is long, arduous and many times painful. The journey is characterized by typical developmental symptoms associated with the in-between stages of *Dissonance, Resistance & Immersion,* and *Introspection.* Some of the indicators of these stages include:

Strong Need to Maintain Cultural Traditions

Many immigrant families will voice the need to maintain cultural traditions. I call this a "need" because of its function to fill a gap that has been created by the experience of lack of belonging through prejudice. Threat to the sense of self leads to a psychological drive to retain a sense of self-continuity by retrieving to a secure base or a holding environment.[2] Idealizing and maintaining cultural traditions is a secure base that is easily accessible to an immigrant in a foreign land. It is the retraction to that which is familiar—like food, dressing, or worship.

Sue and Sue, writing about social enclaves and maintenance of cultural traditions states that many immigrant families find that holding onto their cultural traditions gives them a source of identity in a context that threatens to rob them of identity.[3] There is a familiarity that feeds the psychological need to belong when one can cook meals as they always did at home or when they speak their language.

While on the conscious level this may be deemed as a valuation of their own culture above the foreign culture, its function to feed the threatened sense of self should not be underplayed. Cathecting to this need can become detrimental to children when parents demand that children appreciate these traditions as much as they do. Such demands overlook the fact that these traditions may mean absolutely nothing to children who are growing up in the western context!

For many families, maintaining their cultural traditions becomes almost an obsession to contrast the feeling of insecurity in the foreign majority culture. For instance, many parents will simply ignore the Western

2. Winnicott, *Transitional Objects and Transitional Phenomena.*

3. Sue and Sue, *Counseling the Culturally Diverse.*

developmental stages of being sixteen and beginning to date, or turning eighteen and being defined as an adult, demanding that their children pattern their parents' development. I remember thinking how absurd it would be for me to see my sons holding hands and kissing at sixteen! Those are things that if we engaged in at that age in our African context, they were not meant for the parents to even know! I have also never been comfortable displaying public affection for my husband or receiving affection from him in public because that is just not African, especially not in front of my children.

Displays of affection adored in the West as an expression of love, can easily be termed as crossing of boundaries between parents and children or age groups in Kenyan culture. The response of most families to such cultural expression is a resolution to deepen their commitment to maintain their traditions. Such strict worldviews and age demarcations limit the extent of what one is able to do for recreation with their teen and young adult children. For instance, for many parents it becomes increasingly difficult to go to the movies with their teen children because of fear of the movie having nudity and other age inappropriate language and scenes!

Social Enclaves—Depleted Communal Life

When the immigrant person gets re-defined by the new society as having less value and status sometimes with ridicule and non-appreciation of their giftedness, they, like any other human being, retreat to their social enclaves. In other words, they tend to only socialize in circles where they feel comfortable and appreciated. For most immigrants, this means their social circle is their fellow immigrants usually from the same country/continent. These social enclaves often breed a psychological bias where everything that is foreign in the new culture is de-valued and everything that is familiar and culturally accepted is cherished and protected. To cherish and protect may indeed require the formation of select groups of people where one can truly be oneself and relaxed, while the other (majority or even minority groups that are unlike the self) may be seen as untrustworthy. It is not uncommon to hear children of first generation immigrants who are at various identity stages wondering why their parents do not associate with other parents or frequent social hangouts as do parents of their friends in the majority culture. Parents may associate with majority culture friends either through workplace, church and other necessary social relationships, but these hangouts are essentially different in terms of psychological safety emotional freedom, and other qualitative indicators of open relationships. In more extreme situations, the immigrant family becomes socially isolated especially in geographical areas where they have less contact with their own country people. Their children are essentially caught in between this di- chotomy of social clusters and can easily find themselves isolated because they do not necessarily fit in the parents' social enclaves and yet do not fully belonging in the majority culture.

Integrated Religious/Cultural Values

For the purpose of this book and focus, Christianity will be the faith of focus given the editors' familiarity to its spiritual impact. Yet, issues of dis- sonance regarding spiritual matters about children of immigrant families are not confined to Christianity. Insights of spiritual dissonance discussed here may have similar implications for Islam, Hinduism, Buddhism and other world religions.

We have noted a major difference between Western Christianity and non-western Christianity. This may come as a surprise to some readers for whom the claim that Christianity is Christianity since it is premised on the teachings of the Bible. However, we also know that the Biblical teachings and mandates are contextualized by interpretation of the word. Further- more, Christianity in the non-western world has spread mainly through oral culture than the written word. Hence, its appropriation to the moral, traditional, and cultural value makes it difficult to conclusively distinguish between what is cultural and what is religious. In most non-western con- texts, religion permeates the lives of people so much so that a meaningful distinction cannot be made between that which is religious and that which is social. Mbiti, writing from the African perspective, claims, "to be human is to be religious."[4] Though speaking of the African traditional religion, this is the very understanding with which Christianity was appropriated in the life of the African, such that the line between the sacred and the secular is very thin or non-existent. Religion, and for those who are Christians, Christianity, is therefore so intertwined and ingrained in the life of the first generation African Christian Immigrant, whether he/she professes the re- ligion or not. Hence, the values and morals which guide their being are also held with such sacred significance. The immigrant's world is therefore perceived and experienced through the eyes of religion. Experiences are

4. Mbiti, *Introduction to African Religions*, 108.

explained using religious terms and understandings. Meanings are made through religious beliefs and symbolism. This is a very different perspective from the Western analytical world where everything is first analyzed and scientifically explained.

Such interpretations and meanings have huge implications with regard to what immigrant parents teach their children and how they respond to their children's developmental behaviors and struggles. It is for instance not a surprise to see an immigrant parent experiencing what he or she terms as disrespect from their child, resigning to an explanation that "it is the devil who is trying to attack the family." The solution then must also be spiritual—pray! If one is not a Christian, some families will begin to wonder if they have done something wrong to their ancestors or families at home to warrant these kind of attacks. Sometime they may even voice these meanings to their children in the heat of the moment and I can only imagine what a child who does not have religion as the reference to explain the world thinks of such response to their struggles. Further insights on the effects of spiritual dissonance among first generation immigrant's children might be regarded as *moral-value* issue that affects immigrant teenage identity crises. The phrase *moral value* in some ways captures the totality of third level identity crisis and its unique characteristics. The difference between how laws, morals and values are transacted in the West and non-western communities, lays the main foundation of critical dissonance that leads to unique identity crisis for the first generation immigrant teen and their families.

As already discussed in chapter 1, there is a distinction between laws and morals and values as the guiding vehicles of relationships in the Western and non-western communities respectively. In the West, morals and values are transmitted mostly by one's family. In some cases, institutions such as the church and other faith-based institutions may also influence which morals and values are transmitted. Laws on the other hand are judicial and set apart from morals and values in the West. Laws are written and can be easily referenced, and cited in the judicial system. They apply to all adult members of the society and can be used to coerce required behavior. Because of their power to enforce punishment and consequences, laws in the Western world are powerful in directing behavior.

Among non-western cultures however, morals and values are the guiding standards of normality. In many cases, laws organically spring from morals and values and if a law cannot find a place within the communal moral and value standards, they could very well be dis-regarded as non-functional. They are meant to elicit feeling and emotion, and thus lead to the formation of what psychologist refer to as the super ego. Heinz Kohut recognizes that the formation of the super ego or the moral structure of our being is a transaction of the internal maturity and external impartation of guidance from parents through idealization of the parental system. In other words, the child internalizes the realistic ideals of the parents into the developing psychic structure of the super-ego. In adult personality the super-ego is the important component of our psychic organization that holds up to us our ethical and moral guide—or rather the ideals that hold us accountable to behavior. In Kohut's words, the super-ego "leads to the building up of those aspects of the super-ego which direct toward the ego, the commands and prohibitions, the praise, scolding and punishment that formerly the parents directed towards the child."[5]

The difference in the communal societies is that such impartation is not just directly from the parental system but rather a wider circle of influencers in the moral formation, including extended family and clan members. Indeed, this wide circle of influencers goes as far as to invoke the spirit world of ancestors long gone but whose heritage remains an influencing factor for the family. It is not new to hear an immigrant parent say to the child, "you must always remember that your grandpa's spirit lives in you, live up to his name," or something close in the name of teaching some moral value to the child.

By guiding standards of normality, morals and values thus determine normal behavior and psychosis. For instance, respecting one's parents and seniors is one of the shared highest moral standards in the non-western world. Similarly, while the phrase "children are to be seen and not to be heard" is widely accepted in the non-western world, it is often misconstrued in the Western world to mean denying the child a right to voice or freedom. Rather it points to the expectation that the child must show his/her parents due respect. Even if the parents are wrong, the child should still find the most humble way to bring this to their attention but not blurt it out as though in the same social standing as the parent. Similarly, the saying "*it takes a village to raise a child*" may be conceptually used in the West, but is very practically applied in the non-western world, meaning, children can be corrected and even disciplined by any non-parental adults.

---

5. Kohut, *Analysis of the Self*, 41.

This moral–value versus legal conflicting worlds are a root for the dissonance experienced by children of first immigrant parents and leads to what we are referring to as the third-level identity crisis. The ensuing paragraphs discuss several features of the third level identity crisis as experienced by children of first generation immigrants. We wish to mention that these aspects are not necessarily exhaustive of the teenage experience since such experience varies from teen to teen and may be further varied by factors like: parental assimilation of western culture; parental adherence of spiritual faith; child's sibling order; family location in the north America; age of child's exposure to western world; family proximity and level of interaction with other non-western families; level of parental cultural identity and sense of self.

Identity Dissonance: Who Am I?

As stated in the general identity crisis development, one of the major questions that sparks identity crisis is the question "whom am I?" This is the question that ignites teenage exploration of family narrative, personal looks, substance, gender, etc. For the minority teenage in the US, the question has the rider of who am I as an African American, Asian American, Native American? The same rider is rarely an issue for the Caucasian teenager whose ethnicity is the default for the United States. Such questions will generally bear the aspects of race, color and history associated with one's ancestry. For the teenage child of first immigrant parents, the question bears the third layer rider of "why do my parents (family) behave, believe, and have requirements so different from all my other friends' parents around me, both parents of color and Caucasian? What does this make me? What makes this or that wrong when we all agree it is not illegal? With whom should I hang out? Why do my parents deter my company of friends just because they do things differently? Why do my parents have "mistrust" of other families who do not look like them? These are all questions rooted in one's identity according to beliefs and morals that the child is beginning to sort out for themselves.

The inner crisis is ignited by the fact that when the child looks at him/herself in the mirror they see a likeness of parents, but the feeling inside approximates that of their friends and friends' parents more than their own. "Who am I?" is a loaded question that points to all kinds of inner turmoil for the child of first generation immigrants and a question that continues to plague them as they negotiate the various stages towards adulthood.

Living in Two Worlds

Questions of "who am I?" lead many immigrant children to learn to live in bifurcated worlds. To keep peace at home, they learn the expectations, values and morals of their parents. They follow these as closely as possible and thrive on heaped praise from their parents for exemplifying good character and virtues.

The journey to this amicable seeming compromise is however long, tedious and painful. In most cases, there have been experiences of painful fallout with parents; arguments, denouncements, warnings and seemingly unfair consequences. Pain of depression and feeling alone is very common. Experiences of feeling different, hating oneself, being ridiculed and failing to fit in are also part of this journey. At the juncture they reach this point of compromise and resignation to follow the ways of the parents, for the child it is most likely a resignation to never be understood, while for the parents it is a manifestation that at last the child can see their way. Hence, it is not necessarily the amicable sense of fulfillment that it seems on the surface. Indeed, this juncture may be characterized by occasional lapses to arguments, and disregard of parental direction. To the parents this is termed as disobedience, and disrespect while to the child it is yet another fling at asserting Western individual freedom. The reality is that while the child has learnt what pleases the parents and cues in to these, he /she also has their foot in the other western world of individuality where what matters most is what he thinks and wants as long as it is not legally violating any one. For instance, many children will not argue with their parents about a certain issue being forbidden as a family value—but they will do it any way behind their parents' backs. While general literature on identity crisis may point to similar experience with Western children, the difference is that with the Western parents, as long as what the child is involved in is not illegal, the parents believe that it is up to the child to make that decision and live with the consequences. In other words, it is okay as long as the child can amicably live with his/her own decision. There is no question for the child developing feelings of shame or guilt and therefore no particular danger to developing internal distress and psychosis based on his/her differing views with parents. The parents may express disappointment but are not as invested emotionally. For the non-western parents however, engagement in what has been forbidden as a moral value is regarded as a moral failure. Its consequences are far-reaching in effect to the larger family and even community. Due to such far-reaching effects, the consequence on the child's sense of self is huge. In some instances, the parents not only express their disappointment but also manifest grief and despair over what they think is moral failure on the child and a parental failure on their part.

Furthermore, this sense of failure is communicated to the child if not by word, by gesture, body language and temperament of the parents. Issues of guilt and shame become a pestering part of the child's conscience. This in turn affects the dynamics of the family system in terms of communication patterns, stress, and greater sense of doubt by the parents about their own responsibility in nurturing their child. Many parents question their own parenting styles and responsibility in child's feelings of dissonance. Families find themselves caught in a self-defeating cycle of fluctuating confidence, uncertainty in parental expectations and standards, cycles of harmony and disharmony with teenage children, and fear of the unknown in an unknown country.

With regard to the first generation immigrant children then, the very experience of living two selves: one for the parents' expectations and the other for the individual self can be a source of dissonance and depression. It further distances the child from experiencing a sense of continuity in their own identity. Referring to the four-stage model espoused in chapter 1, the child may find him/herself arrested in a vicious cycle between the *foreclosed* and the *moratorium* quadrants. The older the child gets and cannot move forward from these cycle, the more dissonance s/he experiences, and the more disillusioned and lost s/he feels.

Peer Pressure to Conform to Majority Culture

One of the main hallmarks for teenage identity crisis is the competing voice of peers against that of parents. This is an experience across the board whether one is Caucasian, of color or a child of an immigrant. However, what needs to be noted at this point is the unique driving force that children of immigrants experience during this period of peer pressure. A contextual scenario here is insightful. While for most of the other pre-teen children the parents are the best thing that could happen to them, the first generation immigrant child's relationship with the parents has already been dented. Many children of immigrant families lose their admiration of parents around this age as they begin to compare their families with those of their friends. For instance, many of Hispanic families who have come to the US in search of better jobs and income to sustain their families, rely on their children as the main interpreters of the English language. Most parents are fearful of enrolling in English as Second language (ESL) for various reasons, including the fear of losing their own language by learning a new one, or the fear of being exposed to harsh immigration laws. Their children are therefore occasionally pulled out of school to help interpret for their parents at the banks, social services and even in medical matters. Even where an institution offers interpretation services, many Hispanic families will trust their children for more accurate interpretation because of the history of prejudice, discrimination and general mistrust of the majority culture. While children will obligingly offer these services to their non-English speaking parents, they begin to sense that their family is different and inferior. Their admiration of their parents compared to those of Caucasians begin to dwindle. In a similar fashion, for instance, children of African immigrants, lose their admiration of parents as they begin to sense the inferiority complex that the African parents likely manifest, an aspect associated with cultural identity development and the remnants of colonization as discussed in chapter 1 under the subtitle racial minority identity development. Even where parents are confident and courageous in the face of majority culture, the children make their own meanings about the status of parents' heritage. After all, the society around them including social media, mission work and political rhetoric shows works of charity by the Americans, usually directed towards Africa and other third world countries. Even where parents actively teach their children and expose them to the richness of their culture either through videos, actual visits or stories, the ravages of poverty, disease, hunger and land pollution cannot escape the eye of the child. Indeed, amidst the glorious stories of countries of origin, are the realities of parents supporting their family members financially! While such gestures speak of charitable hearts of their parents to the children, the fact is not lost to the children that unlike their friends' grandparents who spoil them with gifts and vacations and money on their birthdays, and other special occasions, theirs is a reverse. The teenagers also view their parents as un-savvy in navigating the culture they presently live in. For a teenage child whose focus developmentally is the self, this is not a welcome realization about his family. The teenager may love the parents sincerely but simultaneously experience shame in association with them and thus seek to psychologically distance themselves from the family. One can see why peer pressure for the immigrant child becomes a readily welcome alternative to the less admired parents. The need to be accepted by the peers as one who is at par becomes almost obsessive. The more this peer pressure engulfs the child, the more the child tries to seek independence from parents whom s/he views as inferior in knowledge of the American culture. Conflict and constant collision between child and parents become inevitable. The greater the constancy of such conflict the more the feelings of disillusion and dissonance to both the parents and the children, and the greater the possibility of life long rifts between them. Though the examples given here of how such adverse rifts may come about are from Hispanic and African families, other immigrant families are not exempt from such dissonance.

Lack of Clear Role Models

Most first generation immigrants in the US are cut off from their families of origin and the larger extended families. A few of these families may have very tight ties with their homeland and may keep regular contact with extended families especially in the present age of communication technology that includes skype, zoom, tweeter, telephones, instagram, emails, etc. However, very few will ensure that these ties involve their children as well. If the children were born in the US there is a sense in which they are disconnected from infancy. Many parents will try to get conversation going between their family at home and their children in North America, but then language becomes a barrier. I am reminded of a noble idea my husband and I had for our children to be connected and learn our mother language. The opportunity presented itself that I would be gone to South Africa on an academic sabbatical for three months while our children were still young. So we thought what a great opportunity to have their grandmother come and stay those three months so that they can learn the language and have some emotional connection with her. She came and stayed three months. The twist was that she ended up learning English while they did not learn any Meru language whatsoever. Emotional connection? Yes, a little, but it was soon eroded by the distance and the children's irregular visits to Africa.

There is also lack of common interests on which to converse. Many parents try the occasional phone call or skype with extended family outside of the US. However, unless this is an intentional and regular effort, it soon gets ineffective because the two have no common grounds for a conversation. Hence, the simple act of living away from their homeland cuts off the most natural role models that the extended family may offer. Yet we know the importance of role models within the family. For instance, we always hear people referring to a great grandparent or uncle or aunt who inspired them in one-way or another. For the immigrant child, that is not a practical avenue. The child may see pictures, have an occasional word or two on phone with an extended family member, but they do not translate to life-size influence that is so important in creating role models.

As already discussed earlier, the parents are also not the most popular role models. The child is left to find role models in the society either through sports, Hollywood or political icons—who in some ways are also not exactly the mirror likeness to the child because of his/her feelings of being different as an immigrant's child. It is not a wonder that the first generation immigrant's children usually experience a sense of lack of clear direction and ambition in terms of who they are, what they want to do with their lives and who they look up to for inspiration.

Spiritual Dissonance

The first generation immigrant parents who have grown in contexts where religion totalized their entire being—thinking, meaning making, behavior and choices—engender the same perspective as they bring up their children. However, their children are growing in a context where the religious and the secular are intentionally separated. The child is learning from school, teachers, sport coaches, friends, church and politics to live in a world of spiritual/secular dualism. When confronted by syncretism, the child is left in confusion and does not understand why the issues in discussion which seems purely an issue of logical analysis, bears a religious conviction in the mind of the parent. The child cannot understand why the parents are stressing so much on a choice that rests on their own logical analysis and conclusion. Meanwhile, the parent is stressing not because they do not see the logic of the child but because the issue at hand does bear a sacred significance and can have far-reaching consequences for the child and the whole family. Such misunderstandings can become a significant issue between parent and child when the child knows they can put up a logical argument about why they should be allowed to do what they wish as long as it is not harming another. For the parent, such insistence is perceived as defiance, and in many cases, moves against the religious foundation of obeying and seeking guidance of parents. One child, sharing with me their dilemma with parents stated, "*I am twenty-two and an adult. Yet you have no idea the kind of guilt I feel every time I go to buy a beer!*" This I believe is not an action that any Western young adult would have dilemma and dissonance over because it would not be an issue that has been communicated to them with sacred connotations. However, it is talked about by most immigrant families and this is exacerbated if the child is still living at home with the parents, a norm among immigrant families.

In a similar way, immigrant parents have been known to interpret disobedience, and the embrace of what they consider as immoral values, not just as defiance but also as the influence of an external entity. In Africa as well as some Asian cultures, such would be easily characterized as the influence of an evil spirit. This may sound very strange to non-western parents because it almost sounds like a parent is pronouncing their child as evil. Far from it! It has more to do with the religio-cultural intertwined-ness of religion and culture in interpreting life events as already discussed than it has to do with a negative perception of their child. For most non-western cultures, that which cannot be explained rationally, the default is to go to the religious spiritual world. The irony of this situation is that the more the child of first generation immigrant parents struggle to find their identity in a unique emotional wrangling crisis, the more their parents become convinced that they are under the influence of an evil spirit. The more the parents insist on perceiving the child's behavior and choices as influenced by an external entity, the more the propensity of the child to engage in the undesired behavior as they experience isolation, dissonance and even show signs of mental illness.

Conflicting Stages of Rites of Passage

One of the most recurring patterns we find across cultures is the difference between parents and children in how developmental stages are perceived. While not necessarily unique to immigrant families, it seems more pronounced because of cultural differences. Take for instance the year sixteen, popularly referred to in the West as "sweet sixteen." What makes this "sweet" for many western kids is that they can now apply for an interim driver's license, some get their first cars, others can now begin to date, go to their first prom, and given extended curfew hours to hang out with friends, etc. The prom (which comes with being spoiled with an expensive dress and a dance,) becomes part of the rite of passage for this stage. These are experiences many western parents look back with some nostalgic feelings.

Posing these sentiments to a non-western parent and asking them what "sixteen" meant in their experience growing up, many would venture that it was anything other than "sweet!" If they were living in a refugee camp, it meant greater responsibility to help parents care for the younger siblings or find work to help support the family. If they were young girls in the developing world, age sixteen might signify that they had become marriageable and under pressure to find a suitable partner to help escape the poverty at home. Where dowry is practiced, a poor family may look at their daughter's marriage as a potential source of monetary income. For others, this age brings them to a rite of passage whereby males (or in some cases females) might be circumcised and secluded to be given specific instruction of what it means to be a young adult woman or man and the responsibilities of raising a family.

Age eighteen is another good example to show the disparity in cultural markers. In the Western world, turning eighteen means that legal and social support systems now regard you as an adult. At this age, young adults can now buy controlled substances like tobacco; they can file their own taxes; they can differ with the wishes of their parents—and the legal system will recognize their wishes. They can drive with full license; they can even marry. While some of these same realities may be true in the non-western world, eighteen is not the magic bearer of adulthood; rather, it is the manifestation of responsibility. This adult responsibility is measured by relational rather than independent standards such as: respect shown to others in society, logical thinking that takes into account the well-being of the family or com-munity, proper communication of feelings including respect for those older than oneself, fair treatment of the opposite gender during conflict, initiative in education and future vocation. These are the markers of adulthood for most non-western communities. If a teen is not exhibiting these or other traits that the community upholds, they are not considered to be an adult ready to face the world or raise their own family. Age is nothing but a guide signaling around when these real indicators should be attained.

Movement through these ages creates a growing source of anxiety and conflict among children and parents of immigrant families. Each passage may involve numerous negotiations in the family with frequent fall outs and the felt impact exacerbated if it is perceived that these are relatively

easy transitions for American families. Indeed, the mere act of argument
with parents at this age may be deemed as a sign of immaturity and a lack
of readiness for adult privileges and responsibilities!

The manifestation of dissonance and internal conflict brought on by
these rites of passages differ from individual to individual. The differences
are however, more pronounced by the distinction made so well by Agwu
Chinaka[6] regarding first generation, 1.5 generation and second generation
children, as already discussed in chapter 1.

Though presented here as a source of dissonance both for the children and the parents due to their differing perspectives of the developmental stages, we believe that rites of passage have the power to help the
child and parents integrate the two words amicably. They are therefore
the focus of chapter nine as an effective mode of intervention among immigrant families.

6. Agwu, *Acculturation and Racial Identity Attitudes.*

II

Case Studies and Research

3

Children of African Immigrants

Tri-level Identity Crisis from the Perspective of a 1.5 Immigrant

—MERCY LANGAT

"WHERE ARE YOU FROM?" That is an all too common question that I often have a problem answering. "Liminality" seems to be my answer these days. Victor Turner defines liminality as "neither here nor there . . . betwixt and between the positions assigned and arrayed by law, custom, convention, and ceremonial."[1] Turner coined this term while describing the process of rites of passage but I found it to be fitting especially as a 1.5 generation African immigrant.

My family and I moved to Jackson, Mississippi, in 2004. I was almost thirteen years old at the time. I went through culture shock as most immigrants do when they first move to the United States. I was homeschooled for a few months because we moved in the middle of the school year then finally joined eighth grade when the next school year began. Reflecting back, my middle and high school years were filled with struggles of attempting to learn the "correct" way of speaking English, understanding the culture and finding where I belonged. There were a handful of African students in my High School and it seemed like there was an implicit acknowledgement that we were walking through the same journey, so friendships developed. We often discussed amongst ourselves how African Americans, who were the majority in the High School, often accused us of selling their ancestors into slavery. My African friends and I took the role of representing Africa and correcting the all too common negative African narrative. I remember being asked questions such as "do you live in trees?" "Why are you not as

1. Turner, *Ritual Process.*

black as other Africans?" And "did you run with elephants and lions?" I distinctly remember the moment I realized that being an African meant being primitive, poor, dirty, and disease stricken.

All this encouraged me to change and become more "American." The first thing I changed was the main thing that most Americans explicitly or implicitly found to be problematic: my accent. I spoke British English, which is the one learned in Kenya. The main difference between my African friends and myself was that I would switch back to my Kenyan-British accent whenever I was talking to Africans. I intentionally learned the Southern US American way of things so that I could be accepted and in the process, there was a cultural disconnect between my church, school and home life because all those spaces were distinctly different.

College brought about interesting experiences as well. I went to a small, private college in Northern US America that was predominantly Caucasian. Up until then, the only place that I had truly experienced being a minority was at church because my family was the only Black family. I had heard that Black people were minorities but I hadn't made sense of it until I went to college. I tried to connect with African Americans because I had learned to maneuver through such friendships while in high school but there was no real connection. I then decided that it was time to reconnect with my Kenyan heritage and there happened to be a big population of Kenyans close to my college. I attended Kenyan fellowships, Bible Studies, church and other informal gatherings. However, my attempt to connect with the Kenyans was at times met with a cold shoulder because they thought I was "too Americanized." I found myself trying to prove that I was indeed a Kenyan and I would do so by keeping up with Kenyan news, and learning more about the culture.

I also made a point of visiting Kenya for the first time after seven years of living in the United States. That was a monumental trip, because I was in the process of figuring out my identity and connection with relatives and friends in Kenya reaffirmed my identity. Being in Kenya also showed me that I had become "Americanized" in some ways because I experienced reverse culture shock. When I came back to the United States following the visit to Kenya, I quickly noticed that it was easier for me to slip back into the American way of life than it had been to my Kenyan heritage. I continued to grapple with the discontent of "not being enough of Kenyan or American" until I went to graduate school. That is when I was introduced to Turner's idea of liminality and applied it to my experience. I am living in between two cultural identities and I am able to do so because I am a 1.5-generation immigrant. The process of getting to the point of living in between two cultural identities comfortably was quite challenging. It reached a point where it deeply affected my sense of identity because I felt as though I didn't know who I was or am. It was a long journey to where I am now able to appreciate both cultural identities and see their benefits.

These experiences of conflicting identity are at the backdrop of this research. This topic is important because "international migration is one of the greatest issues of this century. . . . We have entered a new era of mobility" that has been enabled by the growth of technology and globalization in general.[2] Furthermore, there has been a steady growth of migration to the United States since 1965 when the US Immigration Act was passed and by doing so removed the national quota system. The demographic of immigrants to North America changed as well. Research shows that "significantly more Asians, Africans, and Latin Americans began moving to the United States" whereas prior to this Act of 1965, the higher percentage of immigrants were European migrants.[3] As migration continues, so does the need to find out the issues faced by each generation of immigrants. This paper examines the differences emerging between the first, 1.5 and second generation African immigrants in the United States. I will discuss the African Diaspora in the United States, issues faced by each generation and the role of the church in assisting immigrants through the acculturation process.

The African Diaspora in the United States

It is important to first establish what is meant by the term "diaspora" and who is considered as being part of the African Diaspora. Most people associate the word "diaspora" to the dispersion of Jews that were in captivity. According to Dufoix, "It doesn't refer to the historic dispersion of the Jews who were taken as captives. . . . It always meant the threat of dispersion facing Hebrews if they failed to obey Gods will, and it applied almost exclusively to divine acts."[4] Dufoix adds that later on the name changed to

---

2. Pocock, *Diaspora Missiology*.

3. Pocock, *Diaspora Missiology*, 6.

4. Dufoix, *Diasporas*, 4.

"designate both the scattered people and the locale of their dispersion."[5]In this paper, the diaspora is considered to be a

"stable community of people of similar ethnic roots who voluntarily or involuntarily live in a foreign locality different from their original environment who have reinvented and reconstructed cultures and social institutions (sometimes religious) and identities complementary and compatible to their host nations which permit them to exist in the new place while having strong links to their homeland."[6]

This definition includes all people that migrated voluntarily or involuntarily. "Diaspora" is also used to categorize people such as African diaspora, Muslim Diaspora etc.[7] The term "African Diaspora" is fairly new; it emerged with writers such as W. E. B. Dubois and was used along with the term "Pan-Africanism" to bring African people together.[8] It is a bit more complex to clearly define who is part of the African diaspora because there are different ideas of what comprises "Africa" and "Africanness." The term at times includes Caribbeans, Haitians, African Americans and those who generally describe themselves as black. In this paper, I consider such people to be Black diaspora. Okpewho and Nzegwu consider the African diaspora to be "all those peoples dispersed from the continent in historic and contemporary times who have constituted themselves into diaspora."[9] However, I consider the African diaspora in the United States to be immigrants from the continent of Africa who can remember or maintain ties to Africa.

History of African Migration

There are many factors that contribute to the migration of Africans to the US. Some factors are changes in Africa such as unrest in respective countries due to ethnic clashes, economic hardships and political climate. Whatever the factors might be, the number of Africans migrating to the US has continued to increase. In fact, "more Africans than the total number that were brought involuntarily to the United States as slaves have settled in the country."[10] They consist mostly of refugees, sojourners and students who believe that there

---

5. Dufoix, *Diasporas*, 5.

6. Nwoji, "Missional Status of African Christians in Diaspora," 9

7. Rynkiewich, "Pacific Islands Diaspora Studies."

8. Nzegwu and Isidore, *New African Diaspora*.

9. Nzegwu and Isidore, *New African Diaspora*, 35.

10. Arthur, *African Diaspora Identities*, 5.

are more opportunities for them in the US than in their own countries. They also tend to be highly educated people, usually working as engineers, doctors, professors, nurses and other professionals.[11]

There are several reasons why Africans migrate to the US. Arthur notes that most research focuses on linking migration of Africans to globalization, colonization, internal displacements, failed nation states, and demand for both skilled and unskilled workers. However, he acknowledges that there is a recent recognition among scholars studying African migration "that education and cultural literacy are poignant factors in modeling the determinants of African migration. Africans have always placed a premium on education."[12] Africans are instilled with the importance of education because it is seen as a means of access to high incomes, jobs, higher standard of living and social mobility. Indeed, education is seen as the vehicle to escape poverty, disease and conflict. Governments believed in the importance of educating their citizens as well. Following the end of colonization, most countries sponsored citizens to pursue higher education.[13] Therefore, education is one of the main reasons why Africans migrate to the United States.

There continues to be a tendency for educated African immigrants to look for job opportunities in the United States once they complete their education. Research indicates, "82 percent of Africans who go to the United States arrive with student visas . . . upon graduation and completion, 90 percent of the Africans will engage in some form of practical training to gain experience in their fields of study."[14] It is during such training that many of the African workers' giftedness is affirmed and opportunities for further development opened. Many of the employers recognize the talents and work ethic that these highly educated professionals offer and take opportunity to engage them. Some workplaces are able to sponsor visas that enable educated African migrants to work in the US and later go through the process of becoming naturalized citizens. Indeed, there is a serious case of brain drain that affects most African countries because African migrants gain jobs, high income and social mobility in the US.[15]

11. Hume, "Ethnic and National Identities."

12. Arthur, *African Diaspora Identities*, 38.

13. Arthur, *African Diaspora Identities*, 38.

14. Arthur, *African Diaspora Identities*, 50.

15. Arthur, *African Diaspora Identities*, 50.

On the other hand, there has been an increasing number of Africans who migrate involuntarily particularly as refugees. The US Code defines refugees as "any person outside of the US . . . who has a well-founded fear of persecution on account of race, religion, nationality, membership in a particular social group, or political opinion."[16] Conflict in places such as South Sudan, Nigeria, Democratic Republic of Congo, Rwanda, Burundi and Somalia has increased the number of refugees entering the US. In fact, a Pew research article indicates that of all the refugees admitted to the US in 2016, the largest number were from Democratic Republic of Congo.[17] The refugee's experiences are quite different from those who voluntarily choose to migrate in search of higher education.

Defining Terms

There are various terms that have been used to describe different generations of immigrants. While the terms serve as a means of recognizing immigrants' identity, it is important to remember that identities are not stagnant. They at times change depending on the level of one's acculturation and assimilation. For example, an individual who migrated with the parents at the age of ten can identify him/herself as a second generation especially if the individual does not speak the mother tongue and rarely has any connections with the parents' country of origin. Studies indicate that children become involved in the new culture quicker than their parents especially if they attend school. School offers the social-cultural vehicle for faster acculturation. "Parents may never acquire sufficient comfort with the new language and culture to become socially integrated into their new country."[18]

The three types of immigrant generations often studied by researchers are the first, 1.5, and second generation. The third generation is often studied as well. However, this chapter focuses on the first, 1.5, and second generations. According to Agwu, the first generation individuals were born in a foreign country. These individuals were also citizens of those countries before they migrated to the United States. For our purposes an additional tangent to

---

16. Igielnik and Krogsad, "Where Refugees to the US Come From."

17. Igielnik and Krogsad, "Where Refugees to the US Come From."

18. Birman and Poff, "Intergenerational Differences in Acculturation."

definition of first generation immigrants is that they migrated to the United States as adults with already formed solid identity.[19]

Rumbaut and Ima first coined the term 1.5 generation in 1998 and defined them as those born in foreign countries but migrated abroad after school-age but before adolescence.[20] Rumbaut later identified the different categories in the 1.5 generation based on individuals age during migration for example, "1.75ers (ages 0–5), the 'classic' 1.5ers (ages 6–12), and the 1.25ers (ages 13–17)."[21] Recognizing the different categories is quite important because each category of immigrants has different experiences. However, for our purposes, we will stick with the classic 1.5 generation immigrants.

Finally, the second generation refers to children of the first generation immigrants that were either born in the United States or migrated with their parents before the age of five.[22] Agwu's definition of second generation immigrants is particularly important because scholars often consider second-generation immigrants as those only born in the United States. Agwu seems to acknowledge child development in his definition. A child who migrated between the ages of zero to five will remember little, if anything at all, about the country he/she migrated from. Therefore, it is appropriate for that individual to be considered a second-generation immigrant even though he/she was not born in the United States. However, a major differentiation between second generation immigrants born in the US and those that came before school age becomes pronounced as they become of age.

It is also important to note that while the word "generation" is used in the terms, it does not necessarily refer to genealogical generation. One immigrant family consisting or two parents and two children can have all first, 1.5 and second generations depending on the children's ages during the time of migration.

Issues Faced by Each Generation

The challenges faced by each generation are often unique due to the process of acculturation. Acculturation is "described as the process of cultural change and adaptation that occurs when individuals with different cultures

19. Agwu, "Acculturation and Racial Identity Attitudes."
20. Inez, "Deconstructing the American Dream."
21. Inez, "Deconstructing the American Dream," 51.
22. Agwu, "Acculturation and Racial Identity Attitudes."

come into contact."[23] These challenges are not culture shock even though it can be included. Rather, they often affect an immigrant's identity. This section will discuss some of the issues that are faced by each generation. There are also issues that are similar to all groups and they will be discussed as well. The issues are not exhaustive but serve as a comparison.

First Generation

The first generation often deals with acculturative stress, lack of power and invisibility. Acculturative stress refers to "a stress reaction in response to life events that are rooted in the experience of acculturation."[24] The factors that contribute to acculturative stress in the African diaspora are separation from family members, lack of community, redefining worldviews and generally maneuvering through a new culture. This is particularly harder for immigrants who migrate with younger children because they leave a society that assists in raising children as the African saying goes, "it takes a village to raise a child."[25] When these parents migrate to the United States, they are required to adapt to an individualistic way of life quite different from their own. Adewunmi also points out that they have to find emotional and functional equilibrium between holding on to their language, cultural and religious practices or adopting their host country.[26] This leads to a lower mental health status exhibiting confusion, anxiety, depression and feelings of marginalization.[27]

This is often more challenging if the immigrant has children because they often do not have power or control over what is adopted and what is not—particularly if the children know the hosts language better and are helping the parents navigate through the culture by being interpreters. According to Agwu, "immigrant children often have the freedom to choose which parts of their home culture they wish to practice. Parents of immigrant students often find little support to help their children incorporate aspects of their home culture with the host culture."[28] While the parents might initially welcome this, it later might become a problem. The first generation immigrants

23. Adewunmi, "Acculturation Stress," 28.

24. Adewunmi, "Acculturation Stress," 29

25. African proverb—source unknown.

26. Adewunmi, "Acculturation Stress."

27. Agwu, "Acculturation and Racial Identity Attitudes," 18.

28. Agwu, "Acculturation and Racial Identity Attitudes," 19.

typically want to maintain their values and cultural traditions. It might be harder to revert back to these values and traditions after the children have assisted them in the acculturation process; the children will have already adopted some values of the host country. The African parents' attempt to impart African culture and norms to the children compete with the childrens' North American peers, socialization and friendships formed at school.[29] The first generation at times lacks power in this area.

The first-generation immigrants deal with invisibility. In his book, *Navigating the African Diaspora*, Carter introduces readers to the anthropology of invisibility. In it, he examines the lives of the African diaspora and concludes that they struggle with social invisibility in their host countries. He describes how difficult it is for immigrants to be registered in the official census records and exclusion from some public spaces.[30] He further describes this invisibility as systemic "perpetual marginality" where by various social orders are implemented so that immigrants continue to be excluded. This exclusion can be seen in educational and work settings; African immigrants tend to be marginalized in those settings. Invisibility is often humbling for most African immigrants to the United States because most of them had careers and were known in their former communities before they migrated. Entering into a new culture where one is invisible and marginalized requires psychological adjustments.

1.5 Generation

There isn't much research done on the 1.5 generation when compared to the first and second generation of the African diaspora. However, the research that has been done on this population points to identity issues as they often have their feet in two cultures, which calls for the need for psychological adjustments. The 1.5 generation often identify themselves as African but could also pass for American; Africans see them as American while Americans see them as African. The tension of being in between two cultures can be referred to as liminality.

Another identity issue among the 1.5 generation is racial consciousness. The first generation goes through this as well but it is particularly challenging for this generation. Racial consciousness begins the moment the individual realizes that they are considered Black in the United States.

29. Awokoya, "'I'm Not Enough of Anything!'"

30. Carter, *Navigating the African Diaspora*, 5.

49

This is a big adjustment because Africans, except for a few countries, do not identify themselves by skin color; they do so using tribes and clans. The African diaspora associate Blackness with being an African American. Therefore, they resist being considered black.[31] This identity is often contested until when the individual realizes that all brown skinned people in America are considered black people even if they are not African American.

Second Generation

The second generations find themselves socialized in the American culture but still acquire some aspects of their parents' heritage culture.[32] They are more likely to identify themselves as Americans because of lack of ties with their parents' heritage culture. Some of them might consider themselves "Kenyan American," "Zambian American," and so on. In doing so, they acknowledge that they don't share the same history with African Americans and it also speaks to the influence of their parents' heritage culture. In other words, by using these specific terms for self-description, they claim and they acknowledge their specific heritage.

The second generation also faces tension with their first-generation parents. In a study done by Butterfield, she found that the parents socialize their children according to their home country while the children assimilate to the host country. The children naturally adopt the host country's values and thus experience tension with the parents. The "children internalize the North American culture and identify and reject their parents' culture and identity as foreigners."[33] This creates lack of understanding between the first and second generation but the 1.5 generation understands and is able to see past the tensions because they have a foot in both cultures.

Similar Issues Faced by All Generations

There are some similar issues faced by all three-immigrant generations. The two that will be discussed are the construction of blackness and stressors. Even though there might be one particular generation that mostly deals with the construction of blackness, all three generations have to wrestle

31. Asante. "Becoming 'Black' in America," 47.
32. Abouguendia, "Acculturative Stressors, Ethnic Identity."
33. Butterfield, "Big Tings a Gwaan," 12.

with it to some degree; the same goes for stressors as well. The 1.5 and second generation have stressors even though it might not be like the acculturative stressors that the first generation deals with.

The 1.5 and second generation African tend "to experience a conflict in their process of constructing blackness based on the perspectives of their African born parents on one hand and the expectations of their American born Black peers on the other."[34] In the childrens' attempt to fit in, their peers' construction of blackness takes precedence. In fact, most second generation might reflect on how they don't understand how they cannot be black because they look black.

Even though the discourse among the first generation immigrants is to adhere to their homes cultural traditions and norms and "downplay their racial identity in favor of their ethnic identities," they still face the issue of construction of blackness.[35] At times they try to avoid it all together by distancing themselves from African Americans. According to Abedi-Anim, there are four reasons why Africans do so. Africans see themselves as sojourners; an "exit option" to go back to their home countries is available to them. Indeed, one of the most common saying used by most Africans to refer to this exit strategy is literally translated as "*it is not storming in Africa*," or "*we did not burn down our homes when we left*," to denote that they still have a solid home and identity in Africa. Second, Africans might distance themselves from African Americans because they are treated "better" by Caucasians. They, therefore, "hold on to their ethnic and cultural identities as a way to gain favor from Whites, especially Whites in positions of power."[36] Third, Africans restrict their identity when they identify as African Americans. This is heightened by the view that African Americans are at the bottom of the racial hierarchy in the United States. Finally, the main reason why Africans distance themselves is because they do not want to be associated with African American stereotypes.[37] Over time however, most Africans that have successfully gone through the identity development which unfortunately starts much later in their adulthood as compared to the same process begun in adolescence by African Americans, realize that the "better" treatment by Caucasians is simply a preference of their stereotyped demeanor of being more accepting and less

---

34. Awokoya, "'I'm Not Enough of Anything!,'" 94.

35. Awokoya, "'I'm Not Enough of Anything!,'" 94.

36. Abedi-Anim, "Bound by Blackness," 5.

37. Abedi-Anim, "Bound by Blackness," 5.

threatening than the stereotype challenging African Americans. Africans soon discover that the "better treatment" offered Africans is actually patronizing of the Africans by the Caucasians.

As previously mentioned, each generation faces some kind of stressors that relate to psychological well-being. A study done by Odera reveals that second generation immigrants go through higher levels of depression than the first generation whereas the first generation had higher levels of self-esteem than the second generation.[38] Therefore, the second generation is more likely to suffer from mental issues related to self-esteem and depression such as anxiety and psychosomatic symptoms. The study further indicates that the second generation might desire to know and identify with their parents' heritage community but might feel alienated due to being less familiar with the customs.[39] The second generation also faces more stressors stemming from tensions with their first generation parents. This is because the disproportion of acculturation between the children and parents is high; the higher the disproportion, the higher the stress.[40] Another study indicates that the first generation experience stressors from communication barriers, loneliness, fear of deportation, career and financial setbacks.[41] This is more evident among those who migrated due to career opportunities.

There is lack of research on stressors among the 1.5 generation. However, one can imagine that the feeling of being stuck between two cultures can be a stressor. Indeed, it can be viewed as a positive thing but it is an identity process that begins with feeling as though an individual is "not enough of anything." Of all the three generations, the 1.5 generation probably has less stressors due to the fact that they understand the American culture and their parents' heritage. The have more connections with their parents' heritage than the second generation and they also have connections in the host country. They can traverse both cultures with a command of some fluidity. However, there is inadequate research within this particular group.

---

38. Odera, "Acculturation, Coping Styles," 73.

39. Odera, "Acculturation, Coping Styles," 73.

40. Odera, "Acculturation, Coping Styles," 73.

41. Adewunmi, "Acculturation Stress."

Role of the Church

Most immigrant response towards stressors is to rely on their faith in God and to find communities where they find a sense of belonging.[42] Perhaps this is because the majority of African immigrants to the United States are Christian.[43] As mentioned before, most Africans migrate to seek job opportunities and to further their education. While pursuing their endeavors in the United States, they also begin churches or become part of African churches. Nwoji states that the African diaspora in the United States participate in reverse mission, social transformation, reaching the Africans in diaspora and mission back to Africa.[44] The church serves as a place where the African diaspora can find a sense of belonging. They can worship together in a way that they are accustomed to; they can find spiritual, relational and emotional nourishment and they can also keep connections with their home countries through mission back to Africa. African churches in the United States also assist immigrants with getting settled and welcoming them into the community.

There are some African churches that intentionally plan events such as camps for children and youth. This might be an avenue where the 1.5 and second generation can find a sense of belonging if there are peers with the same experiences. There is limited research on the church's response to each generation of immigrants. However, it can be inferred that most churches respond to the first generation more than any other generation. Perhaps a better place for the 1.5 and the second generation to build community is through Christian organizations outside of the church such as, African Christian fellowships and African Christian Student Fellowships. There are also some organizations that are specific to a nationality and state, for example, Kenyans in Kentucky, Somali's in Minnesota, etc. According to Ombaba, such organizations are established to seek "to rebuild the community from their home and pass on an African legacy to their children."[45]

The African Christian Fellowship currently has 50 chapters in the United States. The fellowship is made of Africans from various countries and is therefore not homogenous. The fellowship is quite structured having board of directors, representatives and a voting body. They also have

42. Adewunmi, "Acculturation Stress," 72.
43. Nwoji, "Missional Status of African Christians."
44. Nwoji, "Missional Status of African Christians."
45. Ombaba, "In a Foreign Land," 76.

membership but one has to be twelve years of age or older to be a member. They have annual conferences where they invite various speakers, musicians and plan mission trips to Africa.[46] They also intentionally plan activities for children and youth based on ages. Ombaba, a second generation immigrant[47], describes her experience of attending the fellowships by saying "fellowship was the only place besides my uncle's house that I could meet other Africans. It was another world very separate from my school life. . . . It taught me how to socialize with and show respect to African people."[48] Such fellowships serve as a connection to Africa for all immigrants including the 1.5 and second generation.

As globalization continues, so will the migration of Africans into the United States. This migration strengthens the global church because the center of Christianity is shifting to the global South. This migration of people from the global South to the United States strengthens the Christian church as a whole. "The church in America faces the challenge of living into a new kind of community that reflects and honors the global nature of diversity"[49] They can offer hospitality to the African diaspora, identify the acculturative stressors and assist in alleviating the stressors by offering practical assistance and counseling. The study conducted by Odera that showed higher mental health (maladaptive) issues among the second generation is a cause for concern. Therefore, they need a church or people that aware of issues associated with migration and can offer counseling. The emphasis on the American church offering counseling is intentional because at times an outsider can objectively see where the problem lies.

The African diaspora churches should also find ways to integrate the 1.5 and second generation. While passing on the culture, traditions and norms, it is also important to be aware of issues that these two generations in particular face, and identify ways in which they feel included than end up feeling alienated. The issues faced when adjusting to another culture can affect an individual's identity. Therefore, the African diaspora should continue on with their African norm of building community and looking after each other because that is the main way with which stressors

46. Ombaba, "In a Foreign Land," 76.

47. The African Christian Fellowship that Ombaba researched and attended is the same one that I was a part of when my family moved to Jackson, Mississippi. She and I met in that fellowship. Most of the Africans in my high school were members of this fellowship.

48. Ombaba, "In a Foreign Land," 83.

49. Scott, "To Welcome the Stranger," 250.

can be dealt through Ubuntu.[50] In other words, Ubuntu simply means humanness, social unity, community belonging and/or social connections in caring for each other.

50. The idea of "I am because we are." It implies the importance of humanity and living in community.

4

Children of Asian Immigrants

—Sam Kim

On April 16, 2007, there was a shooting at Virginia Polytechnic Institute and State University in Blacksburg, Virginia. It was named the Virginia Tech massacre, and it was "the second deadliest shooting rampage in US history."[1] Thirty-two people were killed and twenty-nine were injured from this incident. The criminal was Seung-Hui Cho, who was twenty-three years old and a senior at Virginia Tech, majoring in English. He was born in South Korea in 1984, came to the States, and became a permanent US resident in 1992. It was quite a shocking crime to the US society as well as the Korean American community.

As the first generation of a South Korean immigrant family, his family was a typical example that showed all of the general issues that Korean immigrant families encounter. Cho's parents were very hard working and spent a lot of time outside the home. As with other children of immigrant parents, Cho and his sister were lonely and did not receive much care from their parents after moving to the States. At school, he was often bullied by his peer students because of his minority ethnic status.[2] As most Korean and Korean immigrant parents have an overly high level of drive for their children's education, Cho's parents had great expectations for Cho's educational success. Although he went to Virginia Tech, his mother was not satisfied and often said to others that she wanted him to go to a more prestigious Ivy League school such as Princeton University.[3]

1. "Virginia Tech Shootings Fast Facts."
2. Gomez-Jurado, *Mad Movie*.
3. Sun Choi, "Why Did Seung-Hui Cho Kill 32 People?"

56

A significant Korean immigrant collectivist response to the Cho shooting incident was quite noticeable at the time. As the criminal was identified as a South Korean, some Korean immigrant parents became afraid to send their children to schools. Korean parents feared that their children would be bullied or retaliated against by their Western peers because of being Korean as was Cho. Some Korean Americans felt their reputation had been damaged as a minority group living in the US, and others showed a repentant attitude because of what Cho as a Korean had done. Most of these Koreans did not know Cho personally, but they felt some kind of connection with Cho's incident because of their common cultural and ethnic identity.

The Korean immigrant adolescents, especially 1.5 and second generation, live under the influence of two cultures: the majority, host US American (i.e., White in this paper), and a minority ethnic culture.[4] In this article, I briefly research the general common background of Korean immigrant society in the United States, issues related to the teenagers of Korean immigrants, and how these factors affect these teenagers' identity development and causes of their identity crisis.

Demographics

The history of Korean immigration to the United States dates back to 1903 (or 1900) and most of the first immigrants worked on the sugar plantations in Hawaii.[5] However, today it can be said that if the first immigrants came to the States to earn money, the many Koreans nowadays come for better education and the future for their children, since the social environment in Korea tends to be competitive.

The total population of Koreans in US is around 1,822,213[6] and of this number approximately 33 percent are adolescents.[7] Nearly half of the population is located in three states—California (535,994), New York (156,386), and New Jersey (109,258). Looking at counties, L.A. county has

---

4. 1.5 generation of immigration means those who were born in Korea and came to the USA in their early age. Second generation means that they were born and grew up in the USA.

5. Han, "History of Korean Immigration to the United States."

6. "Korean Population in USA."

7. "Issues of Adolescence."

the biggest Korean population (over 217,260), followed by Orange county (over 91,468)[8]

Confucian Values and High-Context Culture

Confucianism is considered a foundational principle of Korean people's behavior. No matter what kind of religion people have, Confucian morals and teachings are the basic codes of conduct for individuals and societies in Korea. For centuries, Confucianism has influenced East Asian regions as an essential ontological and cognitive foundation. When it comes to Korea, Confucian ideas governed the society for over 630 years since the Joseon Dynasty (1392–1897). Since then, Confucian values, such as "humanity, righteousness, courtesy, and knowledge" have been embedded in every aspect of Koreans' lives.[9]

Broadly speaking, " 和, Wha," "harmony" is emphasized in the teachings of Confucianism.[10] "Harmony" can be a substantial idea to maintain communal societies such as Korea, China and Japan. In particular, Confucianism sets out five important mutual relationships of ideal human society. With the attitude of seeking the welfare of other people and propriety of the right thing to do at right time, the father should treat his child with "kindness" and the child should show "filial piety" to his father; the elder brother must display "gentility" to younger brothers and younger brothers must show "humility" to their elder one. Husbands must show "righteous behavior" to their wives and wives must show "obedience" to their husbands. The elder shows "humane consideration" to the junior and the junior shows "deference" to the elder. Lastly, the ruler should show "benevolence" to his/her subjects, and subjects should show "loyalty" to their ruler.[11]

Confucian teachings highlight the importance of family. Confucius said that the security or peace of a nation derives from the integrity of the home: 修身齊家後治國平天下, *SuSinJeGaChiGugPyeongCheonHa*. In this sense, ancestor veneration is strongly related to maintaining familial traditions and family members' welfare. If something bad happens to the family or a family member, one of the biggest reasons is because they did not respect their ancestor. Furthermore, women are not considered equal

8. "Increase of Korean population."

9. Yun, "Fun & Easy Guide."

10. Markham and Lohr, *World Religions Reader.*

11. Winfried, *Neighboring Faiths.*

to men in social status according to Confucianism. Women are required to be modest in their personal lives, obedient to their husbands or parents, and are responsible to take care of their family. Women in Confucianism can be depicted as a symbol of the persistence or sacrifice for making an ideal Confucian home and society. Daughters of such families may have experienced parents' or elderly grandparents' discrimination on treating male siblings better than themselves. Sons are considered more important because they continue the family name or line and can take care of parents physically and financially. Traditionally, women are identified through the husband's family name. The daughter in the family is the first to be sacrificed in such issues as to giving up on advancing in education or other opportunities, especially if the family is poor.

Many apparent features of Korean culture such as collectivism, hierarchy, interdependence, and high-context culture have derived from Confucian teachings. For instance, in a hierarchical culture, the way of treating people and use of languages is based on seniority, gender or status. Especially, respecting an elderly person is expected. Even an age difference of one year is considered as senior or elder brother and sister. When strangers introduce themselves, the first thing that they want to know, (other than their names,) is who the senior is in age and the status, because people want to treat others with appropriate respect.

The interdependent relationship between parents and children is also shown throughout the entire lifetime. In general, adult children become independent when they marry. Until adult children are independent, they live with their parents and depend on financial help from them. Later, when the parents are old, the children live together with their parents and take care of them financially and physically. In the past, it was naturally expected that the elder son or only son's family would live together with parents.

Regarding the high-context culture of much of Asia in contrast to low-context culture of Westerners, Koreans have the tendency to communicate in an indirect manner so as not to hurt the feelings of others in order to maintain good relationships. High-context culture needs strong relationships with strong feelings of connection or shared information and environments, so direct confrontation with others is not natural. On the contrary, in low-context cultures, verbal communication is important.[12] In Korean families, if children use a direct confronting message to

12. Hall and Hall, *Understanding Cultural Differences*.

their parents, they are considered very rude and have no respect for their parents at all.

Struggles and Crisis of Teenagers

Identity formation involves integrating a person's personality, and in this time, positive and supportive social conditions and interactions are pivotal. As Erik Erikson stated, identity conflict often occurs among adolescence, between the ages of twelve and eighteen.[13] During this period, how they interact with family, peers and others is essential in constructing their identities and understand themselves.[14]

In worst cases, an identity crisis can bring social dislocation. Actually, some of these issues have surfaced among Korean immigrant adolescents. *Hanho,* a newspaper published for the Korean immigrant community, reported that one of the serious issues that the Korean immigrant society faces is the increase in crimes among Korean immigrant adolescents. They demonstrate anti-social behaviors such as excessive drinking, smoking, taking drugs, and even joining Korean youth gangs.[15] In addition, some Korean immigrant adolescents suffer from depression, anxiety and other mental problems. Minjeong Kim and others researched 138 Korean American adolescents from California regarding their mental health issues in 2016. The results of this research showed that 18 percent of Korean American adolescents experienced significant mental health issues and 23 percent of them showed clinically significant situations. They "also experienced high levels of social problems, thought problems, and attention problems," from adapting to the new culture, as well as "discrimination and changes in social support or income."[16] This phenomenon might be caused by stress and pressure from both inside and outside the home in the process of adapting to a new social context. The difficulty in integrating two very different cultures can lead these Korean teenagers into confusion regarding their identities.

---

13. Erikson, *Identity.*
14. Markham and Lohr, *World Religions Reader.*
15. "Issues of Adolescence."
16. Kim et al., *Mental Health Problems.*

Reasons: Lack of Communication and Connection

There are, of course, various reasons for the identity crisis among Korean immigrant teenagers; however, one of them is a lack of communication and connection with their parents and peers. First of all, most teenagers of Korean immigrant families have difficulty in communicating linguistically and connecting emotionally with their parents. In regards to linguistic communication, many Korean parents are not fluent in English while their children are not fluent in Korean if they came to the States at a very early age. Therefore, conversations between parents and children cannot go very deep and remains on the more superficial level of simply talking about daily matters. Children can understand Korean only if it is not on complex topics and no Chinese characters are used.

On the other hand, the lack of linguistic fluency in English also exists for Korean young people who arrived in the States when they were older and therefore are behind in English skills when compared to their US American peers. The following is but one example of this phenomenon:

> I moved to the states from South Korea, when I was fourteen years old. The biggest challenge or difficulty I had to face through my high school and college years had to do with English. I always had to work extra to improve my level of proficiency in English, and yet, I always felt a bit inadequate because of the lack of sense of ownership.[17]

When it comes to emotional bonding, it is more complicated due primarily to different worldviews. Regarding Korean parents, most of the Korean adolescents I interviewed stated that the most difficult aspect of Korean culture for them to understand, or agree with, is the traditional approach to hierarchy. For example, Korean adults think that just because they are older their opinions are right and they expect younger people to just obey them and show respect by such behaviors as not talking back. This expectation of the different roles between parents and children comes out of the interdependent and collective culture that the first-generation immigrant parents grew up in while in Korea. Because of this, the parents expect their children to consult with them over everyday issues. The parents' patriarchal attitude, however, makes the children feel disconnected from their parents. On the other hand, the parents may have problems associated with immigration. No matter their educational backgrounds, usually they

17. Hunn Choi, e-mail interview with the author, September 2017.

61

work less skilled and less reputable jobs compared to their counterparts in Korea. Therefore, many parents have low self-esteem because of the new living environment, language and culture.[18] Sometimes they want their children to recognize and honor the sacrifices they've made for their children's success, demonstrated by their children's respect for them. For some Korean parents, their children's success is the reason why they are here and why parents can endure all the difficulties. However, when they face their children's independent and individual life style, they are hurt and feel a disconnection in the relationship.

Korean-American adolescents, however, are caught living in an egalitarian and individualistic Western society, their host culture. In adopting and connecting with the host culture, children also experience difficulties and feel disconnected. Interestingly, they consider themselves Korean-American, but if they have to choose one of the nationalities on a cognitive level, their place of birth and/or the age when they came to the States are important variables.

> I think myself as a Korean-American. But if I have to choose one
> of them, then I am American because I was born here.[19]

As a racial minority in the United States, Korean-American teenagers have difficulty entering into the dominant white society. As a result, many of them find themselves not involved fully in either Korean or American society.

Parents play a very important role in the formation of adolescents' identities as the first socializing agents. Korean parents' lack of English skills is another key hindrance to their adapting to, and understanding of, American social customs or the education system. Given this lack of English skills, and shortage of time to spend with their children, some of the first-generation Korean immigrant parents seem to either give up parenting and looking after their teenagers, or are ignorant of their children's struggles and try to control them according to their own cultural values. Although children might need their parents' supports or help, they often end up not receiving it from them. As a result, children often lose respect for their parents and consider them overly demanding with filial duties at home. This can lead to Korean teens having difficulty finding mentors to

---

18. "Issues of Adolescence."
19. GoEun Choi, interview with the author, September 2017

help guide them in matters of daily life which can affect their sense of belonging in either the American or Korean contexts.

Korean-American adolescents live between two quite opposite cultural values and worldviews. Outside home they are required to be more proactive to seek their rights and assimilate to the host culture, but at home they need to be more obedient to the parents and maintain a more collective mindset; it can be very hard for them to integrate into both cultures.

Unique Picture of Korean Immigrant Society—the Korean Ethnic Church

The Korean ethnic church (mainly Protestant and Catholic) is considered a very distinctive institution compared to other national immigrant groups in the USA. Seventy percent of Korean immigrants are affiliated with the Korean church.[20] Koreans often say that whoever meets newcomers at the airport and helps them in their first settling period will decide the newcomers' religion. Most of those who welcome Korean immigrants are Korean pastors and church members who have been in the States and can give advice on how to survive in their new context.

For a long time, the Korean ethnic church has functioned as a social and supportive gathering, and among other things, exchange information on how to survive in the USA. Eating Korean food, celebrating Korean festivals, and honoring Korean values is possible within the church community. The Korean ethnic church serves to give a sense of a "little Korea" and a "pseudo-extended family" for first-generation immigrant members. On the other hand, there are also negative aspects to the Korean ethnic church which could potentially separate and isolate Koreans from mainstream American society, even among other Christian groups. It can limit the use of English, social adaptions, and cause many difficulties for the first generation adult Korean immigrants. However, it also provides a space to celebrate their ethnic identity and exist as a sub-cultural community in their own language and culture.

For Korean immigrant adolescents, it can be a place to experience their ethnic identity and a sense of belonging in the midst of the broader American society. Usually youth meetings in the Korean ethnic church are separated from adult worship services and are delivered in English. This allows the Korean youth to experience both American and Korean cultures,

20. Lee et al., "Ethnic Religious Status."

and to meet their peers who went through or are going through the same issues and struggles. This also provides opportunities to meet life mentors from the church community.

Further Steps for Korean-American Adolescents

How can the confusion in the identity formation process of Korean immigrant adolescents be reduced? The adolescents need to learn new ways of understanding what it means to be Korean-American: "not in-between," "not in-both," "but in-beyond."[21] They may be struggling with an in–between identity and are in the process of integrating both identities, but they need to learn and give a new interpretation to their Korean-American identity for their future. Their unique identity could become an important tool to adapt and live in their multicultural contexts.

So in a practical way, Korean-American adolescents need help to bridge their two identities, to integrate both cultures, and to give a new meaning of being a Korean-American. I suggest that the Korean ethnic church can be one of the places and communities for Korean immigrant adolescents to reduce their identity conflict and to help with their identity development in a positive way because it has existed for a long time among Korean immigrant society and is functioning to connect Koreans to both Korean and American cultural ways. In fact, research indicates that the Korean ethnic church could promote ethnic identity development for the Korean adolescent and at the same time provide a sense of belonging in the American society.[22] Although Korean American adolescents are considered ethnic minorities in mainstream American society, the Korean ethnic church can function as a means for them to experience their ethnic culture, to develop the capability to integrate two different cultures through fellowship with Korean-American peers, and to create hope for their future. In this way the Korean ethnic church might be a positive mediator to help them develop bi-cultural competence. With the correct guidance and positive support, they would come to appreciate and even enjoy their multicultural capabilities.

21. Lee, *Marginality*.
22. Cha, "Ethnic Identity Formation."

5

Children of Hispanic/Latin American Immigrants[1]

—Dinelia Rosa

South America is the Latin American region with fewer immigrants to the US. Mexico, the Caribbean and Central America have higher numbers of immigrants each year. In 2011, nearly 11.7 million Mexican immigrants resided in the United States, representing close to 4 percent of the US population.[2] Mexican-born immigrants accounted for 29 percent (11.7 million) of the country's 40.4 million immigrants in 2011, and close to 4 percent of the US population of 311.6 million. This population has grown twenty times its size since 1960, when about 576,000 Mexican immigrants resided in the country, or less than 6 percent of all immigrants living in the United States in that year. In 2011, about 7.2 million children under the age of eighteen resided in a household with at least one immigrant parent born in Mexico representing 42 percent of the overall population of children from immigrant households.[3] Similar to the overall population of children from immigrant households, the vast majority of children in Mexican immigrant families were born in the United States.

---

1. Editors' note: Some of the contributions in these chapters will show that they were written during a period of immigration that has and is currently changing rapidly. Despite some of the demographics being dated and despite descriptions that may no longer be true given the changing nature of US immigration policy, we believe that the larger dynamics and impact on Tri-level Identity crisis are still very much at play. Therefore we have decided to print these chapters as they were originally written, trusting that our readers will forgive antiquated references, but favor the insights that can still be gained.

2. Stoney and Batalova, "Mexican Immigrants in the United States."

3. Stoney and Batalova, "Mexican Immigrants in the United States."

According to the 2012 American Community Survey 1-Year Estimate, immigrants from South America totaled 3,148,370. Colombia is the South American country with the highest number of immigrants—an average of 658,700 or 24 percent.[4] Colombia's high number of immigrants is the result of the long history of political instability and unrest. Through the end of the 1980s, Colombians living in the US were from upper-middle class and upper-class professionals. However, during the 1990s, less educated Colombians began immigrating to the US as laborers. By the end of the 1990s most immigrant Colombians came to the US seeking political asylum.[5]

The second largest immigration group from South America comes from Ecuador with 435,500, or 16 percent.[6] Most of the Ecuadorian immigrants came to the US as economic refugees. Ecuador experienced a drop in the production of petroleum and significant inflation rates devalued the Ecuadorian currency significantly. Many Ecuadorians reached the US via Panama. Ecuador is followed by Peru with 15 percent and Brazil with 12 percent of the immigrants coming to the US.[7] Overall, as a group, South American immigrants are better educated, less likely to enter the United States as refugees, and more likely to enter as immediate family members than the overall foreign-born population. Despite some differences, South Americans closely mirrored many trends in the overall foreign-born population, including age, arrival period, naturalization rates, and occupations.[8]

The statistics related to Central America immigration to the US are vague and less studied.[9] A significant number of children come to the US alone. The immigration of undocumented children who cross the US border alone has tripled in the recent years.[10] According to recent statistics, most of the children immigrating alone are adolescents between ages fourteen to seventeen, with 77 percent being males. The highest percent of these children (88 percent) come from Central America alone; 34 percent from Guatemala, 27 percent El Salvador, and 27 percent Honduras.[11] These

---

4. US Census Bureau, "2012 ACS 1-year Estimates."

5. USDHS, *2008 Yearbook.*

6. USDHS, *2008 Yearbook.*

7. US Census Bureau, "2012 ACS 1-year Estimates."

8. Stoney et al., "South American Immigrants in the United States."

9. US Census Bureau, "2012 ACS 1-year Estimates."

10. Prah, "Number of Undocumented Children."

11. Statistics provided by the US Department of Health and Human Services in Prah, "Number of Undocumented Children."

three Central American countries are facing high levels of gang violence and many of the adolescents running away from their countries are the sole survivors of entire families murdered.[12]

Reasons for Immigration

The reasons for migration from South American countries varies widely and can be multi-faceted. For example, child migrants from Honduras come to the US due to foreign and diplomatic policy, free trade agreements, global and local economics, and the rampant violations of civil guarantees. In Honduras, this can be attributed to an attack on the education system, an extremely poor healthcare system, poor incentives, violence created by drug cartels that the government cannot control, low wages in export processing zone industries, and a rate of inflation that leaves people not being able to afford quality food and goods.[13] One of the principal problems in Honduras is criminal impunity and the silence of those in charge regarding such violence.[14]

Honduras' homicide rate was 90 slayings per 100,000 people in 2012, the worst in the world and six times the global average. The US State Department warns that a corrupt and toothless police force means "criminals operate with a high-degree of impunity throughout Honduras."[15] Crushing poverty underlies the violence. Nearly two-thirds of the population live below the poverty line, according to UNICEF; one in three infants is malnourished, and children in rural areas get an average of four years of schooling.[16] In the border territory of Guatemala and Mexico there are only twenty-two police officers to patrol forty-three miles of the border and this has shown to be extremely insufficient.[17] For Honduran children the journey means going over this border and into Mexico, and finally to the US. Regardless of the dangerous journey they feel they do not have anything to lose after what they have lost in their country. Many Guatemalan children come from poor rural areas and may be seeking economic opportunities more than avoiding violence. The same is true for children from poorer

12. Ramirez, "More Central American Kids Crossing Solo."
13. Villeda and Zelaya, "Why Are Honduran Children Leaving?"
14. Villeda and Zelaya, "Why Are Honduran Children Leaving?"
15. Gosk et al., *Desperate Journey.*
16. Gosk et al., *Desperate Journey.*
17. Gosk et al., *Desperate Journey.*

parts of El Salvador. For many, the prospect of reuniting with family members in the US is also a powerful motivating force.[18]

The journey for these children includes treacherous and dangerous routes with many adversities. In her bestseller true story, *Enrique's Journey*, award-winning journalist Sonia Nazario recounts the odyssey of a Honduran boy who goes through unimaginable hardship to reach his mother in the US who moved there when Enrique was five years old to send money to feed her children.[19] Enrique's mother kept promising that she would return for him until Enrique stopped believing it and decided instead to go meet with her eleven years later. Enrique did the dangerous trip up the length of Mexico illegally clinging to the sides and tops of freight trains. He faced gangsters that treated him and other children like animals, corrupt policemen that attempted to bribe, and many other undesirable people. Enrique had with him only a telephone number where to reach his mother once in the US. *Enrique's Journey* has become the story of families torn apart, and the story of a boy who risked his life to find his mother.[20] Even though this book was released years ago, this is a relevant book as the influx of minor immigrants coming into the United States has increased and the risks and dangers they faced have multiplied. Many of the children traveling alone suffer serious accidents in the journey such as losing limbs due to falls from the train, girls and boys being raped, and many others dying in the trajectory. Once in the US those that survive are taken to group homes, shelters, or are deported back to their country of origin. Many children returned to their country would take the risk again to travel back to the North.

The emotional reactions that children experience with the unexpected news that the reunion with loved ones will take longer than expected are not recognized or validated once reunited, leaving the child with unprocessed emotional feelings that may contribute to an unhealthy emotional development and adaptation process.[21] The experience of carrying an emotional despair due to separation and the new emotions of reunification are not talked about. Immigrants encounter a sense of loss, grief, and mourning. The process of not being able to talk about the sense of loss and despair caused by the process of immigration has been considered as

18. Gosk et al., "Desperate Journey."
19. Nazario, *Enrique's Journey.*
20. Nazario, *Enrique's Journey.*
21. Falicov, *Latino Families in Therapy.*

a disenfranchised grief[22]—i.e., being disallowed from the right to grieve. From this framework it can be said that immigrant families and children are denied the opportunity to grieve the loss of family, friends and even the land. Parents may think that the children are better off and doing well in the new country and miss the importance of the unprocessed emotional sense of loss and separation experienced by both children and parents. Families are so busy trying to make it in the new land that they miss opportunities to talk about the experience of separation and loss.

How and by whom children are taken care of in the country of origin before they reunite with their parents in the US is another important significant factor with a noteworthy impact on the child's emotional and psychological development. For children, the transition to live with family members or friends means a disruption in attachment from their parents and a process of re-attachment with the new caretaker. Even if they know the person they are now living with, living with the person on a permanent basis is novel and at times strange and confusing. Children are required to go through a process of adaptation and readjustment to the new person and a re-adaptation of attachment connections.[23] The emotional adverse consequences of disruptions in attachment in children are well documented.[24] Disruption in affective bonds has effects on children's behaviors.[25] According to Bowlby, "When a young child finds himself with strangers and without his familiar parent figures, not only is he intensely distressed at the time, but his subsequent relationship with his parents is impaired, at least temporarily."[26] The affective disruption can be displayed in many ways including emotional detachment, or clinginess to the caretaker.

Immigrant children from Central America are treated different from Mexican immigrant children. The US favors them over other children arrested at the border. For example, Mexican children are deported immediately, while other Latin American children are detained and then put in the care of parents or relatives in the United States. They are then assigned a court date, but union leaders of the US Border Patrol agents say many families skip the court dates, and the children join America's population

---

22. Vazquez and Rosa, *Grief Therapy with Latinos.*

23. Vazquez and Rosa, *Grief Therapy with Latinos.*

24. Bowlby, "Processes of Mourning."

25. Bowlby, "Disruption of Affectional Bonds."

26. Bowlby, "Disruption of Affectional Bonds," 81.

of eleven million undocumented immigrants.[27] The children take buses from El Salvador, Honduras and Guatemala, and when they reach the US-Mexico border, they cross alone, with siblings or in groups of children, according to families. To reduce the inflow, the US government is providing millions of dollars in aid to the three Central American countries to combat violence at home: $40 million for Guatemala, $25 million for El Salvador, and $18.5 million for Honduras.[28]

The pathways of these immigrant Latino young adults and children are a general policy concern because of the impact on future labor markets and earnings, as well as the generational impact of low education on children. The Obama administration's recent implementation of the Deferred Action for Childhood Arrivals (DACA) initiative, granting a two-year reprieve from deportation for unauthorized immigrants brought to the United States as children, has added greater importance to this issue in policymaking and educational circles because school enrollment is an essential criterion.[29]

Challenges Faced Once in the United States

Like many other immigrants, those coming from Central and South America have unique experiences navigating the US culture. They experience many challenges in the process of adaptation. Relationships between parents and children go through changes during this process of adaptation to a new culture. Many contributing factors have been cited as making this process more challenging for recent immigrants. Among them is the level of education of the immigrant children. Mexicans have lower levels of education, are more likely to be in the labor force, and are more likely to work in lower-skilled occupations. They currently have higher unemployment rates than other immigrants or US-born workers.[30]

To date, studies on the educational pathways and experiences of immigrant high school dropouts have concluded that their interrupted education (a) reflects structural and economic barriers to school participation; (b) indicates a general disinterest in education; and (c) represents a termination

27. Martinez and Hurtado, "Central American Immigrant Parents."
28. Martinez and Hurtado, "Central American Immigrant Parents."
29. Lukes, "Pushouts, Shutouts, and Holdouts."
30. "Mexican Immigrants in the United States."

of their educational trajectories.[31] An interesting phenomenon being explored recently is associated with declines in educational outcomes across immigrant generations. This has been labeled the "Immigrant Paradox."[32] Educational declines in attitude and behavior across immigrant generations was found to be strongest in schools with more negative peer cultures.[33]

Many factors have been found to correlate strongly with a high risk of school dropout, including low socioeconomic status, disinterest in education, and low achievement. Among participants in this study, school interruption occurred as early as age ten and as late as age seventeen. Although their common feature is an incomplete high school education, two distinct groups emerged in the sample: first, those who interrupted their schooling due to limited financial resources and poverty in their families of origin; and second, those who abandoned their studies when they migrated. A very small number interrupted their schooling due to pregnancy or because they started a family with a partner.

In terms of language, with the exception of Brazil, South America's primary language is Spanish. Brazil's official language is Portuguese spoken by 99 percent of its population. English has replaced French as the second primary language spoken among educated people. Other languages include indigenous languages, and languages of most recent European and Asian immigrants.[34]

The process of acculturation has a significant role in changes experienced in family roles, expectations, and points of conflicts among immigrant family members. Acculturation is the process by which a person comes into contact with a culture different from the original one, and begins a process of adaptation.[35] Family members go through the acculturation process in their own individual way; it is not a uniform process. While some people may adapt quickly, others may do so at a slower pace. Some family members may be very receptive to the changes brought by the new culture, while others may be less receptive creating unexpected family conflicts. What follows is a description of some aspects explored in the literature of acculturation and immigration.

31. Suárez-Orozco and Rhodes, "Unraveling the Immigrant Paradox."
32. Greenman, "Educational Attitudes."
33. Greenman, "Educational Attitudes."
34. US Census Bureau, "2012 ACS 1-year Estimates."
35. Marin and Gamba, "New Measurement of Acculturation."

The impact of traditionalism in the process of acculturation among immigrant families to the US is an area that has been explored.[36] According to the literature, the more traditional families are when they come to the US the more difficulties they have adapting to the new changes.[37] This includes being less open to new social, cultural and religious perspectives. Families may feel a need to preserve their traditional belief systems without having to blend in with the new culture. Immigrants with traditional views tend to show low levels of acculturation as compared to the less traditional immigrants.[38] They can remain in the country for decades without increasing their level of acculturation. This has an impact on children as they are confronted with demands from both sides, to remain loyal to the original traditions versus adapting to the new culture.

According to the acculturation theory, people can integrate both cultures and the more this is possible the healthier and less stressful the acculturation process.[39] Among US Latinos, higher levels of adoption of the American host culture are associated with positive effects on health care use and access. Acculturative stress refers to the psychological, somatic, and social difficulties that may accompany acculturation processes, often manifesting in anxiety, depression and other forms of mental and physical maladaptation.[40]

Generation levels also have a significant role in the process of adaptation and acculturation. Studies show that first generation immigrants tend to be more traditional and less acculturated, while second generation children tend to be more receptive to cultural aspects of the American culture than their parents and more prone to reject some of the traditional belief systems of their parents.[41] Acculturation is also positively correlated with years of education in the US with more years of education in the US showing higher levels of education and greater proficiency in English.[42] Adults whose education was primarily in their original country

---

36. Marin and Gamba, "New Measurement of Acculturation"; Falicov, *Latino Families in Therapy.*

37. Falicov, *Latino Families in Therapy.*

38. Gil and Vazquez, *Maria Paradox*; Marin and Gamba, "New Measurement of Acculturation."

39. Marin and Gamba, "New Measurement of Acculturation."

40. Falicov, *Latino Families in Therapy.*

41. Marin and Gamba, "New Measurement of Acculturation.

42. Marin and Gamba, "New Measurement of Acculturation.

will show lower levels of acculturation as compared with children that came to the US and completed most of their educational years in the US. Children studying in the US are reducing their language barriers as they learn English and put it into practice.

One study explored the link between cultural discrepancy (i.e., perceived acculturation and gender role disparity between children and their parents) and depression among children of Latino immigrants. Compared to boys, Latina adolescents reported greater differences in traditional gender role beliefs between themselves and their parents and higher levels of depression. Gender role discrepancy was associated with higher youth depression, with this relationship mediated by increases in family dysfunction. Gender role discrepancy effects were more pronounced for Latina adolescents. Gender role discrepancy was associated with poorer family functioning for girls but not for boys. These preliminary results point to the importance of considering cultural discrepancy as a contributing factor to youth depression.[43]

The impact of acculturation, and the stress associated with it in immigrant families, is significant. As family members acculturate at different pace and levels, it begins to create differences among them in regards to cultural behavior, practices, traditions and values. This variability may create family disagreements and conflicts, resulting in a lack of family cohesion. Arbona, Olvera, Rodriguez, Hagan, Linares, and Wiesner (2010) conducted a study to examine differences between documented and undocumented Latino immigrants in the prevalence of three immigration-related challenges: separation from family, traditionalism, and language difficulties to acculturative stress and fear of deportation.[44] Participants in the study consisted of 416 documented and undocumented Mexican and Central American immigrants living in two major cities in Texas. The Hispanic Stress Inventory-Immigrant form was used to assess acculturative stress in the sample. Results showed that although undocumented immigrants reported higher levels of immigration challenges of separation from family, traditionalism, and language difficulties than documented immigrants, both groups reported similar levels of fear of deportation. Results also indicated that the immigration challenges and undocumented status were uniquely associated with extra-familial acculturative stress but not with intrafamilial acculturative stress. However,

43. Cespedes and Huey Jr., "Depression in Latino Adolescents."
44. Arbona et al., "Acculturative Stress."

fear of deportation emerged as a unique predictor of both extra-familial and intra-familial acculturative stress.

Another study exploring the acculturative stress during the first two years after immigration found that Latinos with undocumented immigration status, those with lower education levels, and those without family in the US generally indicated less family cohesion and experienced more acculturative stress.[45]

In a study developed to investigate factors that predict acculturative stress in a nationally representative sample of Latino migrants consisting of 2,059 Latinos immigrants from Mexico, Cuba, and other Latin countries—Colombia, the Dominican Republic, El Salvador, Ecuador, Guatemala, Honduras, Peru and Nicaragua, findings revealed that acculturative stress decreased with an increase in the English language, the context of migration, and the social network.[46] Furthermore, acculturative stress was lower for US citizens versus non-citizens; immigrants who wanted to migrate to the US versus refugees who had to leave their country of origin; and later generation immigrants. Acculturative stress increases with a higher native language proficiency, less English proficiency and a higher discrimination index.[47]

A typical example is the difference in which each culture perceives gender and parental roles and the impact of this in Latino families living in the US. In the Latino culture, the male figure is considered the head of the family household. Machismo is a man that has a sense of overprotection for what he considers his property, which may include wife and children. This overprotection is projected by jealousy and control over the wife or female mate. Some aspects of *machismo* are often perceived as negative—an exaggerated sense of masculinity, prowess, and pride, with a sense of men feeling superior to women. Machismo also has positive aspects, such as a strong sense to be the bread-winner and supporter of the family, and a feeling to protect and care for family members.[48] Marianismo, the counterpart of Machismo is also considered part of the traditional role for women in the Latino culture. Women are expected to defer to their husbands or partners, and are expected to be good wives, mothers, and daughters above everything even if this includes self-sacrifice of

45. Dillon et al., "Acculturative Stress and Diminishing Family Cohesion."

46. Lueck and Wilson, "Acculturative Stress in Latino Immigrants."

47. Lueck and Wilson, "Acculturative Stress in Latino Immigrants."

48. Gil and Vazquez, *Maria Paradox.*

their desires as independent women. They are expected to be available for everyone else except for their themselves.[49]

Once in the US these traditional roles are challenged covertly or overtly by immigrants. If the man is the first to immigrate to the US, the mother is placed in a position of authority over her children in their native country, a difference from when the father was in the house. Sometimes a male representative of the father is designated to be the authority figure while the father is away. In both instances the children are faced with confusion while they try to adapt to the family changes. Once the whole family reunites in the US, children are confronted once again with having to reorganize their perception of their parents' roles. The mother that they perceived as the authority figure is not any longer and they are expected to respond to a father that was absent for many years the same way as in the old days. In the meantime, children have grown and many are adolescents that may have some trouble re-adapting to their parent's expectations of how they should respond to the authority figure in their family.

If the mother is the first to immigrate, she is placed in a position of being the bread-winner for the family. Chances are that she sends more money home than what her husband or partner provides. This creates changes in the gender roles with the mother being placed in the position of authority from the financial perspective. The mother becomes independent in the US. Once the family reunites, the expectations of the mother to accommodate to her old traditional family role can be challenging and even conflicting.

Generational differences in women's beliefs about traditional female roles as a result of the shared bicultural experience in the US have been recently studied. One study compared a group of Ecuadorian women living in Riobamba, Ecuador, to a sample of Ecuadorian women living in New Jersey. Fifty mother-daughter pairs in each sample showed that mother-daughter differences about traditional female roles disappear in those women residing in the USA but not in those residing in Ecuador.[50] This study confirmed results previously reported by a similar study done with Colombian mother-daughters.[51]

Family cohesion or lack of it may also be determined by generation status. One study examined how family conflict and cohesion related to

49. Gil and Vazquez, *Maria Paradox*.

50. Lega and Procel, "Acculturation and Generational Differences."

51. Lega and Procel, "Acculturation and Generational Differences."

lifetime service varied by generational status for Latino Americans (n = 2,554) as compared to Asian Americans (n = 2,095). This study showed that first-generation Asian Americans reported greater family cultural conflict than their Latino counterparts, but third-generation Latino Americans had higher family conflict than their Asian American counterparts. First-generation Latino and Asian Americans had the highest levels of family cohesion. Furthermore, Latino Americans who reported higher family cultural conflict and lower family cohesion were more likely to use mental health services.[52]

Religion of Immigrants

In terms of religion, Mexicans and Dominicans are more likely than most other Hispanic origin groups to say they are Catholic, while Salvadorans are more likely to say they are evangelical Protestant than Mexicans, Cubans and Dominicans.[53] Central and South America's religion is represented by Christianity, Judaism and Islam. It is estimated that the largest religion in Central America is Roman Catholicism with 74 percent of the people. The second religion is Protestant with 7 percent. In South America, 80 percent are Catholic and 10 percent Protestant. Argentina is considered the number one Roman Catholic country in the world with 92 percent.[54] Jews in Latin America date back to the expulsion of the Jews from Spain in 1492, and by the sixteenth century, fully functioning Jewish communities existed in Brazil, and countries of Central America.[55] Today, there are 500,000 Jews in Latin America, most of whom live in Argentina and Brazil.[56] The Muslim religion in Latin American countries was spread through immigrants during the eighth to fifteenth centuries coming from Africa as slaves.[57] It is estimated that the total Muslim population by country varies from 4 to 15 percent. Muslims in the Latin countries are not well documented; however, in Argentina it is estimated that there are between 900,000 and one million Muslims. They mainly arrived to Argentina from Syria, Lebanon, and Palestine.

52. Chang et al., "Importance of Family Factors."

53. Krogstad, "Mexicans, Dominicans Are More Catholic."

54. US Census Bureau, "2012 ACS 1-year Estimates."

55. Ruggiero, *Jewish Diaspora*.

56. DellaPergola, "World Jewish Population, 2017."

57. Ali, "Islam Project."

Once in the US, immigrants are influenced by the same religious groups. It is estimated that there are more than 15,000 Spanish-speaking Muslims in the US.[58] Young children become Muslim once in the states. Raymundo Nur, a Panamanian who became Muslim at the age of twelve and studied Islam in Saudi Arabia later went on to help organize the Los Angeles group is an example of how immigrant children are converting. Today, Southern California has the third largest concentration of Muslims in the US, including fifty-eight mosques and Islamic centers in Los Angeles County.[59] If we keep in mind that Southern California also has a big concentration of Mexican and other Latin Immigrants, we can think that they are being exposed to the Muslim religion.

Immigrants converting to a religion different from that of their families can bring confusion, conflict and friction. For example, the case of Dormy Garcia, a Mexican Immigrant, mother of two, shows how her family in Mexico became upset after they learned that she converted to Islam. Dormy shared with them that she let go of Catholicism, the religion that was imposed by her Mexican ancestors and was determined to raise her children Muslims.[60] Once in the US, immigrants feel less pressure to continue with the traditional religion and are more willing to try new ones.

Religion promotes social support, bonding and socialization and a sense of community, but it can also present challenges. In a cross-sectional, qualitative study with 114 adolescents and young adults, Abo-Zena and Barry found that religion and religious contexts served as challenges and resources for immigrant youth with respect to the extent of support they felt they were receiving from church, heritage and/or liturgical language, and contribution and volunteering.[61] Religion has been shown to protect youth from high-risk behaviors such as drug abuse as well as providing behavioral guidance.[62]

Developmental Challenges of Immigrant Adolescents

Developmentally, adolescents go through identity transition from childhood to adulthood. Erikson defined the adolescence stage as a "crisis

58. Ramirez, "New Islamic Movement."

59. Ramirez, "New Islamic Movement."

60. Ramirez, "New Islamic Movement."

61. Abo-Zena and Barry, "Religion and Immigrant-Origin Youth."

62. Abo-Zena and Barry, "Religion and Immigrant-Origin Youth."

identity." During this time, adolescents try to differentiate from their parents and seek to identify with their peers.[63] This struggle becomes more challenging for them when it takes place between two cultural worlds. While they try to differentiate from their parent's, they may not have a solid group of friends with whom to identify. Outside they find diverse groups and peers of various interests that may increase confusion and uncertainty. Adolescents may seek identification with groups similar to their struggles—either Latinos or African-American. Unfortunately, some of these groups are found in gangs.

Immigrant adolescents find it more difficult to engage in social friendship making it harder for them to develop a healthier separation from parents to social groups. In a study aimed at examining patterns of social engagement in friendships and extracurricular activities among racial/ethnic minorities and immigrant adolescents, five measures of social engagement: having friends, socializing with friends, participating in school sports, participating in school clubs, and participating in activities outside of school were analyzed. The study utilized the Education Longitudinal Study of 2002,[64] a nationally representative sample of high school sophomores. Overall, results showed that racial/ethnic minority adolescents, as well as first and second-generation adolescents, were less engaged in friendships than their third generation, White counterparts. These findings suggest that a disproportionate number of racial/ethnic minority and immigrant adolescents are less engaged in friendships than their peers, and that schools and adults play an important role in facilitating social interactions that may not occur within informal friendship networks.[65]

One variation of ethnic identity formation not indicated by earlier theories is described by Rumbaut[66] as reactive ethnicity. Reactive ethnicity signifies a process whereby perceived threats, persecution, discrimination and exclusion reinforces for a person the accentuation of group differences, heightened group consciousness of those differences, a hardening of ethnic identity boundaries between "us" and "them," and the promotion of ethnic group solidarity. Reactive ethnicity may explain why some young immigrants join ethnic-related gangs

63. Erikson, *Childhood and Society*.
64. See NCES, "Education Longitudinal Study of 2002."
65. Cherng et al., "Less Socially Engaged?"
66. Rumbaut, "Reaping What You Sew."

Adolescent immigrants are also increasingly at risk for alcohol abuse. Studies indicate that US-born Latino teens exhibit higher rates of alcohol use compared with their foreign-born counterparts. Different hypotheses have been advanced to explain the mechanisms underlying this phenomenon, including the erosion of protective cultural factors across generations and increased exposure to risky peer environments in the United States. Erosion of family closeness and increased association with substance-using peers mediated the relationship between generation and alcohol use patterns.[67]

Mental illness resulting from the immigration process also contributes in negative ways to the development of adolescents. Pediatrician Alan Shapiro, medical director of Children's Health Fund's in Montefiore-based medical programs for highly disadvantaged kids in New York City, in cooperation with Catholic Charities New York, recently co-founded Terra Firma, an innovative medical-legal partnership designed to meet the complex medical, psychosocial, and legal needs of unaccompanied minors. Shapiro observed that immigrant children's life experience is marked by multiple traumas in their home countries, on their journey north and here in the US. He treats children that have severe post-traumatic stress disorder, and depression.[68]

It is important to mention that immigrant youth and children respond differently to the challenges they face and not all of them present adverse reactions to the adjustment to the US. Many children similarly exposed to the same conditions show resilience and an ability to succeed in school. One factor associated with a positive outcome that predicts the extent to which a child engages in learning the new language, forging new relationships, and connecting academically is self-efficacy or the belief that one is competent and in control of one's learning.[69] Other protective factors include family stability, having more than one adult bringing income to the family, and parental education.[70]

67. Bacio et al., "Drinking Initiation and Problematic Drinking."
68. Redlener, "Undocumented Children Need Charitable Help."
69. Suárez-Orozco and Rhodes, "Unraveling the Immigrant Paradox."
70. Suárez-Orozco and Rhodes, "Unraveling the Immigrant Paradox."

6

Child-Rearing Challenges for Undocumented Mexican Parents in Detroit

—Janet Diaz

This chapter describes the situations of undocumented Mexican Catholic immigrant families living in Detroit. The parents, aged thirty-five to forty-nine, have been living in the US for five to twelve years. All are married and most completed high school in Mexico. None have college educations. All of the parents work outside the home, with both the husbands and wives working forty hours or more per week or more.

Filling out the survey used to gather data as a foundational resource for this book was not an option for these immigrants. In general, the immigrant parents do not have personal access to computers. Although they may be able to access computers in public settings such as libraries, most of them would not have the necessary computer literacy to complete an online survey. In fact, they would need to depend upon their children's help in order to fill out an online survey. In addition to lack of computer skills, the immigrant parents would also struggle to understand a survey written in English.

Some of the parents have teenagers or young adult children who were born in Mexico and emigrated to the US with their parents. None of the family members entered the US with legal documentation. Other parents have both older children who were born in Mexico as well as children who were born in the US after the families' emigration to Detroit. Although the families live in a predominantly Hispanic neighborhood of the city—Southwest Detroit—the children's formal education through Detroit Public Schools occurs entirely in English. Some of the neighborhood small businesses have Spanish-speaking employees and others do not.

The immigrants chose Detroit because of reports that jobs were available there, and also because of the high populations, in Southwest Detroit, of immigrants from their hometowns in Mexico. In many areas of the US, immigrants from particular towns in Mexico tend to congregate in the same US towns. For example, there are many immigrants from the Mexican states of San Luis Potosí and Jalisco living in the Detroit area.

The parents have limited ability in speaking, comprehending, reading, and writing English. Their skills in English range from very little ability to communicate to some rudimentary ability to make themselves understood in English. The older children usually speak English very well but may have a slight accent; native speakers of English would be aware that English is not their native language. The younger children are perfectly bilingual in terms of spoken language and auditory comprehension; however, they are not fluent in reading or writing in Spanish.

All of the parents report economic motivators as their primary reason for leaving Mexico and emigrating to the US. In this sense, "escaping from events at home," (one of the options listed on the survey) could be one accurate way of describing their motivation for leaving Mexico. They were not, however, escaping from "events"; they were escaping from conditions of extreme poverty. Violence created by organized crime—usually drug cartels— was an additional motivating factor for some of the immigrants.

Although these immigrants felt compelled to leave their homeland in order to escape poverty and violence, they also felt great sorrow and pain of separation at having left immediate and extended family members behind. They also miss their hometowns, the familiar customs of home, and the values implicit in the lifestyles they left behind. Because of their undocumented status, they do not enjoy the possibility of occasional visits home. The uncertainty as to when, or if, they will see family members again serves to deepen this pain of separation.

The immigrants also live, to varying degrees, in situations of isolation, since their undocumented status makes them afraid to interact in certain settings where the possibility of apprehension followed by deportation is perceived as high. Many of the undocumented immigrants have a circumscribed physical area within which they live most of the time. This limitation in their movement makes them feel less vulnerable to possible legal actions against them. One single mother, for example, shared that she lives within a four-block square area in Southwest Detroit. Susana[1] described her scope of activity: "Within these four blocks," she said, tracing a circle in the air with her finger, "I have the restaurant where I live and work, the parish, the bank where I go to send money home to my older children, and the grocery store." She and her ten-year-old son live in a one-room apartment above the restaurant where Susana works. Her son, who was born in the US, takes the bus to school each day. She does not visit the school since this would require going outside of the area within which she feels secure; in fact, she has never laid eyes on her son's school. Susana's husband in Mexico abandoned the family. Her ten-year-old son's father, who was Susana's partner in the US for several years, was deported and is now back in Mexico.

The immigrants report a desire to continue working in the US for the next several years. They may seek to return to Mexico at some point, but right now the "when" is an open question and their decisions will be based largely on the economic situations in both countries as well as on their own perceived level of security in the US. While the parents miss their lives and family in Mexico, the children generally feel that Detroit is home, since their interaction with life and family in Mexico has been either limited or, in the case of those children who were born in the US, non-existent. The children's lack of connection with the same memories of and attachments to Mexico is a source of sadness for the parents, who feel that the children do not know, and therefore cannot honor, their roots. Nevertheless, living in a Hispanic neighborhood and belonging to predominantly Hispanic parishes does ensure that the children are regularly exposed to a Spanish-language environment, traditional Mexican foods and celebrations, and religious rituals such as *quinceaños*, masses and commemorations of the feast of Our Lady of Guadalupe.

The García family exemplifies the situation of many undocumented families living in the Detroit area. María and Juan García have been living in the US for eleven years. They have three children—a twenty-three-year-old daughter, who was born in Mexico, and two sons, eight and ten, who were born in the US. Their daughter, Ana, speaks English with a slight accent but speaks fluently and comprehends her second language fully. Both sons, Efraín and Roberto, speak English and Spanish with equal fluency.

Juan works for a company that does landscaping during the spring and summer months and snow removal during the winter. All of his co-workers and his immediate supervisor are Hispanics. As a result, Juan

---

1. All of the names used in this essay are pseudonyms.

is surrounded by Spanish speakers in his work and has had little to no opportunity to learn English. María works in a Mexican restaurant in Southwest Detroit. She too is immersed in a Spanish-speaking, culturally Mexican setting at her place of employment. Even though the couple has been living in the US for several years and both have not only the desire to improve their meager English-language skills but also the understanding that better English skills could help them to "get ahead" in the US, the circumstances of their lives have not been conducive to pursuing this end. Since their undocumented status causes them to be fearful about venturing out of their small scope of their home and workplaces, the possibility of studying English at a community college, for example, is out of the question. Finances would also be an obstacle to taking classes.

Ana graduated from the Detroit public high school which corresponds to their neighborhood. Although Ana would like to pursue college studies, her undocumented status prohibits her from access to federal and state financial aid programs. Since her parents cannot afford to pay even community college tuition rates, Ana is working as a waitress in a Southwest Detroit Mexican restaurant. Efraín and Roberto attend the local public school. All of the children's education is conducted in English. However, since Spanish spoken at home, at church, and in some neighborhood settings, the children are not only bilingual but bicultural.

In addition to work settings that are linguistically and culturally Hispanic in nature, Juan and María are active in a predominantly Hispanic Catholic parish in Southwest Detroit. At their parish, all but one of the weekend Masses is celebrated in Spanish. They participate faithfully in the meetings, retreats, and other activities of the parish Charismatic Prayer Group. In addition to Mass, their prayer group membership and activities are the bedrock of their faith life. Through the prayer group, they study Sacred Scripture, participate in communal prayer and worship, and both organize and participate in retreats through which they gain spiritual sustenance and renewal.

The children participate to different degrees in parish activities. Ana participates in youth group meetings and events at the parish. María explains that her sons are less and less interested in attending parish activities. She attributes this in part to their ages but also to the influences of their peers at school, whose lifestyles and values would not support involvement in religiously oriented groups.

The García family's situation is typical of many undocumented Mexican families in in the Southwest Detroit area. Many families have a mix of children in terms of their birthplaces, with children born in both countries. Parents often are not proficient in English while their children are bilingual. Parents strive to retain, within their families, the values they learned growing up as children in Mexico. The children are caught between two worlds which compete for their allegiance, the traditional Mexican cultural paradigm and the dominant US cultural norms. Parents do not feel "at home" in interacting with the US institutions and systems that have great influence over their children.

One common example is the parents' struggles in dealing with the school system in Detroit. María described her frustration regarding her interaction with her son's school. When she attends the parent-teacher conferences, she depends upon her sons to translate the teachers' comments about her sons' performance and behavior at school. She feels powerless, she reported, since she is never sure whether her sons accurately communicate what the teachers are saying. One of the sons, Roberto, has experienced bullying at school. María shared her feelings of inadequacy in terms of seeking the school's intervention to help with this situation. "I can't communicate well with the teachers or the principal," she said. Meanwhile, her son is resisting going to school and his grades are falling. Finally, she asked her daughter to attend a meeting with the teacher in order to translate. When the teacher essentially blamed Roberto by saying that he was also participating in bullying other children, María felt at a loss to truly understand what was happening and to be able to advocate for her son.

Parents like the García's face several challenges in raising their children in the US rather than in their native country. Some major challenges arise from the parents' lack of proficiency in the English language, their lack of cultural fluency in terms of US dominant culture,[2] and their lack of knowledge about the workings of major institutions, such as school systems, which have a major influence in their children's lives. All of these factors are directly related to the parents' undocumented status in the US. Another major challenge is the lack of access to extended family members, who would

2. At this time, there are many individual cultures which together comprise US culture. In the context of this essay, "US dominant culture" or "US mainstream culture" refers to the culture of most of the middle-class, dominant whites in US society and to the culture that pervades US schools in terms of popular television shows, movies, and social media. The school culture is most readily seen through internet sources and other forms of mass media.

typically play key roles in the raising of children both in terms of the practical help they could offer as well as serving as wisdom figures. Differing views of authority in the US versus their native country also create challenges in terms of the relationships between parents and their children. The children's diminishing appreciation of and respect for Mexican customs and traditions is also a troubling matter for these parents. Some of the most troublesome issues parents face are discussed below.

Raising Children without the Support of the Extended Family

For many Mexicans, family is the foundational construct and support system in life. And unlike Americans from the US who often consider family to be only the closest family members, Mexicans think of family in a much broader sense. First and second cousins, great aunts and uncles, and the families of in-laws would all be within the realm of what Mexicans would call "family." Designations such as "immediate family," "extended family," and "distant family" are foreign to Mexicans and to most other members of Hispanic cultures. For them, family is family, whether the person under consideration is a sibling, a second cousin, or, in some cases, even a very close friend. The idea of "the nuclear family" makes no sense to most Hispanics. Mexican children will often relate to non-related god-parents as closely as they relate to blood relations.

Family constitutes a foundational epistemological base for Mexican children growing up in Mexico, since family is the means through which most Hispanics know about God, the world, and themselves. This knowing is both intuitive, coming from experience within the family, and didactic, coming from the teachings of elders (primarily) and peers. Family is the network of relationships that allows the individual to know and define him or herself and creates the foundation for life. Mexican immigrants in the US will often speak, for instance, about being taken to church by their grandmothers and learning their prayers at her knee. Mention of *abuelita*—an affectionate form of referring to one's grandmother—will usually illicit narratives of tender memories reflecting the foundational role the grandmother played in the person's childhood. They fondly remember annual celebrations not just with their "immediate" families but also at the homes of great-aunts and uncles, first and second cousins, and in-laws.

The undocumented parents, who were raised in a culture in which their own identities were defined in large part through their membership in their family group, try to fill their typical Hispanic need for community and personal relationships with others through new relationships in Detroit. These new relationships consist of friendships with, for example, co-workers, neighbors, or fellow parishioners. While these new relationships may help to assuage the parents' pain of missing family, the new friends cannot possibly fulfill the same needs in terms of child-rearing for their children that their extended family members played in their own growing up in Mexico. The extended family is absent, and it is difficult or even impossible to replicate this type of environment for their children. The *abuelitas* are simply not present, in the US, for the immigrants' children.

The void created by the absence of the extended family is exacerbated by the fact that the two parents often work full-time plus, trying to earn enough money, through their minimum-wage jobs,[3] to sustain their families. Even the parents themselves, therefore, are absent from the home during much of the day. María shared that her sons are home alone much of the time. She is anxious about the presence of drugs, abandoned homes, and juvenile delinquency in the neighborhood, as well as gang members who sometimes visit their street. She also shared her concern that her sons will be lured into "the bar on the corner where women dance naked." Even the young children, she says, dress in sexually provocative clothes. Also, she stated that her sons' friends are disrespectful and use foul language. "This is not how we have raised our children to be," María shared, in a despondent voice.

The role of the extended family in child-rearing is indicative of a fundamental difference between US dominant culture and Hispanic cultures. This difference relates to the emphasis placed on the individual versus the group or community. Hispanic cultures tend to place the good of the group above the good of the individual. "The group" or the community, in Hispanic cultures, is usually the extended family. US culture tends to place more emphasis on the individual; independence and individual achievements are prized and venerated. This focus on the individual, which is foreign to most Hispanics, also contributes to the creation of an environment which is not ideal for Mexican parents raising their children.

The undocumented immigrants' children are immersed, through their experiences at school and their general exposure to US culture, in the approach which emphasizes the individual over the group. This clash

3. Some undocumented immigrants, because they have no recourse to legal action, often earn less than minimum wage and are expected to work extra hours. Many employers of the undocumented have no sense of social justice regarding their treatment of the immigrants, providing no paid vacation or sick time.

of cultures in the children's lives creates problems at home. Esperanza, a mother of a fifth-grader and a seventh-grader, complained that what she and her husband tried to teach the children at home about respecting the good of the family was not reinforced at school. "The teachers are always urging the children to be independent," she said. "My children use this to tell me that I'm different from their teachers and that I'm not helping them to succeed in school. My husband and I feel that the teachers have more authority over our kids than we do," she reported. Esperanza fears that her children will become adults who do not assign the family the central role in their lives.

María complains that her two younger children have been negatively influenced through their experiences at school, specifically in terms of their attitudes towards family and elders. She claims that her sons' friends at school are always pushing for independence from their parents and that this pressure has caused her children to be less respectful towards her and Juan. "They don't appreciate the proper way that children should treat their parents," she says. María is saddened by the fact that she sees no good peer role models for her sons. "All of their friends are just as bad or worse in the way they treat their parents." She explains that many parents feel that they are an embarrassment to their children and that honoring the family is no longer a value for the children, especially the younger children. She feels as though the teachers do not understand, and therefore cannot reinforce, the proper role of the family in their students' lives.

Another mother, Claudia, complains not only of negative influences from peers but also from some teachers. "The teachers emphasize independence," she says. "This pushing the children to be independent is contrary to our traditional family way of life," she adds. A few years ago, Claudia expressed concern to a Spanish-speaking teacher at her eight and ten-year-old sons' school about the boys' incessant fighting with one another at home. The teacher referred the older son to a school social worker who spoke only English. After some sessions with the social worker, Claudia's son became increasingly disdainful of his family and of his parents' involvement in his everyday activities. He eventually explained that the social worker was encouraging him to be responsible for himself and his own actions. According to Claudia, this led to a level of independence that was disrespectful to the family. She felt that the social worker did not understand her expectations of her son and was leading him in a direction that might be positive for the US mainstream culture but was not acceptable in her family.

Because of the lack of extended family in their lives in the US, the undocumented immigrants are at a great disadvantage in raising their children. The traditional support network family would provide is not available to them. The connection to family peers, elders, and to the "hierarchy of wisdom" which the extended family provides, and which inspires the respect of younger family members are all absent.

Lack of Knowledge of US Language, Culture, and Institutions

Many of the undocumented Mexican immigrant parents experience deficiencies in terms of their understanding of US mainstream culture and US institutions. This deficiency is the result of lack of English language skills and of living their lives basically within a Mexican "ghetto" in the US. Because of their undocumented status, they are often unable to avail themselves of services that could improve these conditions. They are locked in a state of permanent liminality, being away from the familiarity and comfort of home and yet unable to fully integrate into the new place.

Since they speak little or no English, the parents feel inadequate in terms of dealing with the school system or with teachers and administrators at school. They have no way of knowing whether their children need special services for conditions such as learning disabilities. Even if they were aware of these things, they would have a difficult time advocating to make sure their children receive the necessary services. They often rely on their children to act as their translators. As mentioned above, they sometimes do not trust their children to accurately translate the messages of teachers or administrators.

For the parents who have older children, they do not understand enough about higher education in the US to be able to guide their children. Although there are services available which might help their children to pursue education at, for example, the local community college, the parents are in unknown territory when it comes to navigating the system so that their children could benefit from higher education.

A good example of the lack of institutional knowledge and ability to make institutions work for the good of the immigrants' children is the recent Dream Act which was passed by Congress. Although some of their older children who entered the US without documents are eligible to apply for permanent residency through this legislation, the parents have little understanding of how to help their children through the maze of legal requirements necessary for the children to avail themselves of this opportunity. Fortunately, some, though not all, of the older children may find sources of help outside the family.

María Guadalupe has been living in the US without documents for nine years. She and her partner Raul have a one-year-old son. When María Guadalupe left Mexico, she left behind her daughter, Verónica, now fifteen, to be raised by her parents (Verónica's grandparents). María regularly sent money home to support Verónica, providing a higher standard of living for her daughter than she could have provided had she remained in Mexico. When her daughter became pregnant in Mexico, María Guadalupe decided she should come to the US to give birth. She borrowed money from, as she puts it, "everyone" she knows in order to pay special, costly *coyotes*[4] that would bring Verónica across the border through means that would not involve the physically harsh and sometimes even life-threatening conditions that most undocumented immigrants face in their journeys from Latin America into the US.

With Verónica in Detroit and about five months pregnant, María Guadalupe struggled with how to best care for her daughter without risking deportation. María Guadalupe discussed her dilemma as to how to handle her daughter's next steps. "I feel that the first thing I should do is take her to the doctor," she shared. "She is four or five months pregnant and has not had any medical care at all. But when I take her to the doctor they will ask me where she goes to school. What will I say? I can get into big trouble if I say she is not in school. Then they could notify the authorities who could come after me and deport me. So, should I enroll her in school first, let her go to school in this state (she motions to Verónica's belly) and then have to wait to take her to the doctor?" For all of María Guadalupe's desire to do the best for her daughter, her undocumented status in the US created a trap within which she felt caught.

Susana expressed frustration over her lack of involvement in her son's education. She does not visit the school where her son studies because she feels at a loss due to her lack of familiarity with school and its programs. Due to her lack of English language skills, she is not able to be involved in activities at the school. In terms of his life at school, her son operates in a very separate world in which she does not feel comfortable.

---

4. "*Coyotes*," Spanish for "coyotes," is the slang term used to refer to the smugglers who coordinate the illegal crossings of emigrants from Mexico to the US. Many *coyotes* are members of powerful cartels.

Other parents reported feeling ashamed within the context of the children's schools because of their lack of English ability. They sense a prejudice, on the part of the teachers, towards them. At the same time, they feel guilty that they are unable to communicate with their children's teachers. Oftentimes those who find themselves in a foreign-language context feel that their inability to communicate is perceived as a lack of intelligence. This feeling accurately describes how the parents feel in many US settings, but most importantly in the children's schools. Some parents consider that teachers and administrators react to them out of racism; this in turn leads them to question whether their children are also experiencing the effects of racism within the schools.

Another consequence of the lack of ability to speak English is the parents' inability to supervise children's homework. A teacher with experience teaching at a largely Mexican Catholic school in the South Central district of Los Angeles reported that parents cannot supervise children's homework. They can neither monitor whether the children actually complete the assignments nor check any completed assignments for accuracy. She added that, even if the parents had the ability to check their children's homework, they probably would not have the time to do so since they spend so much time working.

Lack of understanding of certain elements of US culture also puts parents at a disadvantage in terms of raising their children with the values they themselves learned in Mexico. For example, the parents' lack of technology savvy makes it easier for children to play inappropriate video games. The teacher from South Central expressed her disappointment when she found out that her second and third-graders were watching "The Family Guy," an adult entertainment show, on television. After investigating, the teacher discovered that the parents thought that since "The Family Guy" is a cartoon, it was acceptable for young children. Negative influences both at school and in the neighborhoods draw children to inappropriate music, videos, and TV shows. Because of parents' lack of understanding US mainstream culture and the English language, they are unaware of the need for supervision of their children's activities in these areas.

The lack of cultural and linguistic fluency that could lead to greater family success in the US is a barrier for the Mexican immigrant parents. "I would like for my children to play soccer or baseball," one father shared, but I can't follow the necessary information sufficiently to encourage my kids to get involved." Even if the children did play a sport, he admits, it would be difficult to take them to practices and games, given his demanding work schedule.

Role Reversal

One of the most difficult realties the undocumented immigrant parents face is the role reversal that often takes place between themselves and their children. In this reversal, children assume the role of the parents and parents become like children. Again, this dynamic occurs because of the parents' lack of English language ability and cultural fluency in the US.

As mentioned above, the immigrant parents are often not able to assume their full parental responsibilities in their children's school settings. They are either "in the dark" as to what is happening with their children's educations or they are dependent upon their children to act as intermediaries with tasks such as translating. This situation is a classic example of the role reversal that takes place within the immigrant families.

Additional examples of role reversal include the use of services such as banking. The parents take their children with them to the bank when they need to open accounts. The children do the talking, translating for their parents from Spanish to English and translating for the bank employees from English to Spanish. Any type of computer work also creates situations of role reversal. Since the parents are not computer literate and the children have learned computer skills at school, the children complete any tasks requiring the use of a computer. Shopping is another instance where the child functions as the adult. Since the parents cannot communicate with English-speaking clerks or cashiers, the children again bridge the gap, helping parents to get answers to their questions and to pay for their merchandise.

The parents confessed that the role reversal is a source of humiliation for them. Especially in a culture where the hierarchically-arranged roles of parent-child carry considerable weight, the parents feel embarrassed, especially in public, at having to rely upon their children in these ways. Role reversal erodes the parents' sense of authority over their children, since the parents themselves often feel like helpless children in these situations. Esperanza described a situation in which her daughter grabbed her wallet out of her purse in order to pay a bill in an office. The daughter showed her frustration with her mother's lack of understanding and simply took over, dominating the situation in a way Esperanza found to be disrespectful. The implied disregard for the parent-child hierarchical relationship is painful for the parents; the parents' lack of ability to handle certain situations on their own and can be embarrassing for the children.

The Problem of Materialism

The parents all bemoaned the effects of what they perceive as a highly materialistic US culture on their children. They believe that, if they were raising their children in Mexico, there would be less emphasis on trendy haircuts, brand-name clothing, and expensive athletic shoes. The parents expressed concern that their children's self-images were too closely tied to these external expressions of status. Clothing and other external symbols are also tied to gang behavior, and parents worry that some of their children's choices in terms of apparel might be indications of sympathies towards some gang behaviors,

Whether or not it is true, they perceive that the influence of materialism is stronger in the US than in Mexico, especially in the lives of young people. Their children's demands for expensive clothing, the parents share, place an unreasonable strain on the family budget. Also, the children seem to feel entitled to these "privileges," which is disturbing to the parents. The parents blame US mainstream cultural influences for what they, from a Mexican cultural perspective, consider their children's over-attachment to the material.

Also, the parents view their children's desires for brand-name clothing and other expensive accoutrements as selfish desires which undermine the well-being of the family. With the parents working many hours at minimum-wage jobs, they resent their children's insistence on spending unreasonable sums of money on clothes. Again, the role of the family takes a backseat, as far as the children are concerned, to their material desires.

Conclusion

To a great degree, the parents' difficulties in child-rearing can be traced to their undocumented status and to their poverty. With documentation, parents could have access to frequent visits home to Mexico, allowing the children to develop at least some degree of relationship with the extended family. Also, parents could better avail themselves of certain services which could help them to improve their lives in the US. Lack of legal status goes hand-in-hand with living in poor neighborhoods; poverty creates greater challenges for parents trying to raise their children with traditional Mexican cultural values. Ironically the poverty the immigrants experience in the US is much less severe than the poverty in which they lived in Mexico.

Undocumented Mexican immigrant parents living in Detroit face many struggles in raising their children. There are many negative consequences of bringing up children in the absence of the extended family, which is so fundamental to healthy child-rearing in Mexican settings. The parents' busy work schedules exacerbate the effects of the lack of participation of the extended family. Not only are primary family role models, such as grandmothers not present, but the parents themselves are often away from home. Parents also perceive that the US cultural emphasis on the individual over and above the group has negative effects on their children and makes them less respectful of parents and family in general.

The parents' ability to effectively engage in all the services and institutions which affect their children is compromised by their lack of English-language proficiency and low understanding of the workings of US organizations. Parents are frequently unable to advocate for the best interests of their children because they simply do not know how the system "works." Problems in this area are especially common in the parents' dealings with their children's schools.

Role reversal, in which children act as parents and parents as children, is a common occurrence for these families. This dynamic causes embarrassment for both the children and the parents and can undermine the parents' authority over their children since children tend to lose respect for their parents when they are called upon to act, on a regular basis, in a parental type of role.

The undocumented parents complain that living in the US makes their children more materialistic than they would be if they were living in Mexico. US cultural influences, mainly through peers at school and media, cause the children to place too great an emphasis on outward signs of status. The children's insistence on the material also strains already tight family budgets.

The clash of cultural values which the immigrant parents confront on a daily basis, coupled with their own limitations in terms of their lives in the US, causes great difficulties for families. Along with the typical problems parents often face in rearing children, the immigrants face additional layers of difficulty. For undocumented Mexican immigrant parents in Detroit, raising their children is a constant and complex challenge.

7

Caribbean Immigrants

—Anthony Headley

Introduction to Black Caribbean Immigrants

BLACK NATIVES OF THE Caribbean represent a growing immigrant group within the USA and a number of studies have documented this reality.[1] In 2000, immigrants from the Caribbean represented one-tenth of all foreign-born persons in the USA.[2] Between 2000 and 2005, they comprised some 6 percent of immigrants.[3] Furthermore, among Black immigrants to the USA, Black Caribbean immigrants comprise the largest group.[4] Depending on the source and date, this group comprises between 4 to 6 percent of the Black population in the USA.[5] They represent more than a quarter of Black immigrants on the east coast, congregating in such cities as New York, Boston, Miami and Fort Lauderdale.[6] This growing number of immi-

1. Goosby et al., "Ethnic Differences in Family Stress Processes"; Lorick-Wilmot, *Creating Black Caribbean Ethnic Identity*; Sanchez, "Racial and Ego Identity Development"; Seaton et al., "Prevalence of Perceived Discrimination"; Taylor et al., "Comorbid Mood and Anxiety Disorders"; Thomas, "Socio-Demographic Determinants of Language Transition"; Williams et al., "Mental Health of Black Caribbean Immigrants"; Wilson, "What It Means to Become a United States American."

2. Thomas, "Socio-Demographic Determinants of Language Transition."

3. Guy, "Black Immigrants of the Caribbean"; Thomas, "Socio-Demographic Determinants of Language Transition"; Williams et al., "Mental Health of Black Caribbean Immigrants"; Wilson, "What It Means to Become a United States American."

4. Williams et al., "Mental Health of Black Caribbean Immigrants."

5. Kalmijn, "Socioeconomic Assimilation of Caribbean American Blacks"; Williams et al., "Mental Health of Black Caribbean Immigrants."

6. Goosby et al., "Ethnic Differences in Family Stress Processes"; Kalmijn,

grants from the Caribbean make them an important group worth studying. Notwithstanding these growing numbers, this group has not always received a great deal of attention in the literature.[7]

The immense diversity among immigrants from the Caribbean presents a problem when one tries to introduce this group.[8] Caribbean immigrants are by no means a homogenous group. Besides the high percentage of persons with roots in the African continent, one can easily find Caribbean immigrants from European, Indian, Chinese, other racial background or a mixture of all these.[9] But this group does not simply differ by racial background; they also differ in many other respects including language, geography, and culture.[10] Within the Caribbean countries one will encounter persons who hail from islands largely influenced by English, French, Spanish or Dutch history and language. These realities often make for inter-island differences that go beyond language.[11]

Beyond these differences, each European colonial power brought a history and tradition that dominated the islands. The particular colonial history exerted significant influence on the culture and customs observed within a particular country and these may still be evident.[12] But even here, the colonial history does not fully explain intra-island differences. In fact, many of these islands also have a mixed influence.[13] As a result, an island that originally had a French colonial history may have changed hands at a later date and experienced colonization by the English. This shift in colonial overlord often made for a shift in language and the predominant customs and culture that goes along with the latter experience. At the same

---

"Socioeconomic Assimilation of Caribbean American Blacks"; Sanchez, "Racial and Ego Identity Development"; Seaton et al., "Prevalence of Perceived Discrimination"; Taylor et al., "Comorbid Mood and Anxiety Disorders"; Williams et al., "Mental Health of Black Caribbean Immigrants."

7. Guy, "Black Immigrants of the Caribbean"; Wilson, "What It Means to Become a United States American."

8. Sanchez, "Racial and Ego Identity Development"; Wheeler and Mahoney, "Caribbean Immigrants in the United States."

9. Murphy and Mahalingam, "Perceived Congruence between Expectations and Outcomes"; Sanchez, "Racial and Ego Identity Development."

10. Bridgewater and Buzzanell, "Caribbean Immigrants' Discourses"; Guy, "Black Immigrants of the Caribbean."

11. Murphy and Mahalingam, "Perceived Congruence between Expectations and Outcomes."

12. Guy, "Black Immigrants of the Caribbean."

13. Bridgewater and Buzzanell, "Caribbean Immigrants' Discourses."

time, while influenced by the later colonial power, inhabitants of these countries also maintained some of the culture, customs and sometimes the language of the original colonial power. Such differences described here can often be seen among those persons who share the same racial background. Indeed, there may be significant differences even among those who are of African origin.[14] Given these realities, in studying this group, it is important to acknowledge the varied cultural and other differences that mark this population rather than see them as a homogenous group. Instead, one ought to value Black Caribbean immigrants as a distinct group within the larger immigrant community.[15] Additionally, given these differences, one ought also to be attuned to the different ways in which Black immigrants acculturate to US society.[16]

Impact on the Acculturation Process

These differences exert major influence on the acculturation process of Black Caribbean immigrants to the USA.[17] Acculturation has been described as the process of adaptation that occurs as persons transition from one culture into a second culture. It is a process requiring persons to adapt psychologically and behaviorally.[18] Accordingly, the significant differences in the social and culture history of persons from the Caribbean exert some influence on how people from the Caribbean acculturate to the USA.[19] For instance, given the fact that English is the official language of the USA, it seems reasonable that those persons from the English-speaking Caribbean will likely adapt more easily to this country. This way of thinking is

14. Murphy and Mahalingam, "Perceived Congruence between Expectations and Outcomes."

15. Guy, "Black Immigrants of the Caribbean."

16. Guy, "Black Immigrants of the Caribbean."

17. Archibald and Rhodd, "Measure of Acculturation for Afro-Caribbean Youth"; Guy, "Black Immigrants of the Caribbean"; Jackson et al., "Use of Mental Health Services"; Joseph et al., "Rules of Engagement"; Smith et al., "Serial Migration and Its Implications for the Parent-Child Relationship"; Williams et al., "Mental Health of Black Caribbean Immigrants."

18. Archibald and Rhodd, "Measure of Acculturation for Afro-Caribbean Youth."

19. Archibald and Rhodd, "Measure of Acculturation for Afro-Caribbean Youth"; Guy, "Black Immigrants of the Caribbean"; Jackson et al., "Use of Mental Health Services"; Joseph et al., "Rules of Engagement"; Williams et al., "Mental Health of Black Caribbean Immigrants."

not foreign to the literature on Caribbean immigrants. Indeed, some have pointed to the greater success of English-speaking immigrants than those from other Caribbean groups.[20]

Given this latter fact and the difficulty of trying to grasp the sheer breadth of differences among Caribbean immigrants, I have chosen to focus this chapter on immigrants from the English speaking Caribbean with a particular focus on their children. More specifically, I have chosen to largely focus on those persons of African descent from the English speaking Caribbean. But even here, although there are many similarities, there are also differences. For example, an individual from Barbados may exhibit some differences than persons from another English-speaking country. One significant reason for this difference is that unlike many neighboring countries, the English were the sole colonial power in Barbados. Barbados was consistently British from 1627 onward and was even called "Little England." Contrast this with the colonial history of St. Lucia. This island, though English in its later history, evidently also had a French background reflected today in the continued use of French-based patois while at the same time having English as its main language. A similar pattern can be found in islands such as Dominica.

I have chosen to focus on Black Caribbean immigrants from the English speaking Caribbean for another reason. As indicated by the National Survey of American life (NSAL), 70.1 percent of the Caribbean sample migrated from the English speaking Caribbean. The remaining 29.9 percent hailed from French and Spanish countries in the Caribbean area.[21] Similar numbers among these three major languages of the Caribbean have been reported elsewhere.[22] This large percentage of people from the English speaking Caribbean provides a good rationale for focusing on this group. At the same time, given limited information in some areas, I will sometimes cite data from other Caribbean groups. This is done with the clear sense that information gleaned from other groups will not always be fully relevant to Black immigrants from the English-speaking Caribbean given some of the differences already discussed. Nevertheless, despite the acknowledged differences, similarities also exist that make such an approach somewhat reasonable.

20. Kalmijn, "Socioeconomic Assimilation of Caribbean American Blacks."
21. Jackson et al., "Use of Mental Health Services."
22. Kalmijn, "Socioeconomic Assimilation of Caribbean American Blacks."

Religious Values and Cultural Traditions

In regard to religious values and cultural traditions, there appears to be limited data about Black Caribbean immigrants in the USA. A computer search using a social science database yielded few studies from the USA. Instead, many of the studies addressing these issues derived from British sources and a few from Canada. Given this lack of information as well as the breadth of diversity even among English-speaking Afro-Caribbeans, I will discuss religion and cultural traditions broadly.

From personal experience, the islands of the Caribbean possess a rich history of religious beliefs and cultural traditions. Religion in general and Christianity in particular continues to play a large role in the lives of persons from the English-speaking Caribbean. Indeed, within countries like Barbados, churches are ubiquitous, with the Anglican faith dominating the island. One will also find places of worship that sometimes mix the Christian faith with other expressions, sometimes reflecting African roots. However, the author admits that this interest in religion might be different depending on the locality or country in which such persons live.

One might infer continued interest in religion among Black Caribbean immigrants from the development of an acculturation instrument that included items on religious beliefs and practices. The instrument also included other scales focused on preference for things Black/Caribbean, beliefs and practices related to family and health, interracial attitudes and cultural superstitions.[23] The participants in this study included an initial panel of eight Caribbean youths, who had lived ten plus years in the USA. They helped to modify two other acculturation instruments for use with persons from the Caribbean. Next, the authors utilized five community members who reviewed the instrument. Finally, the revised instrument was completed by forty Afro-Caribbean youth ranging in ages from thirteen to nineteen.[24]

In this study, the authors noted that the items related to religious practices engendered a great degree of discussion in each participating group.[25] Discussion items included feelings of loss relative to some of the religious practices from their African ancestors. They lamented the destruction of their churches, clergy and members whose practices included both African

23. Archibald and Rhodd, "Measure of Acculturation for Afro-Caribbean Youth."
24. Archibald and Rhodd, "Measure of Acculturation for Afro-Caribbean Youth."
25. Archibald and Rhodd, "Measure of Acculturation for Afro-Caribbean Youth."

and Christian practices. In order to survive, over time, they eventual modified their beliefs and practices.[26]

A study of sexual practices among Black adolescents in Canada may also shed some light on the role of religion in the lives of Black Caribbean youth in North America. In this study, Christian religions dominated the various groups from the Caribbean and Africa. To a lesser extent, some youths from Africa identified themselves as Muslim.[27] For the most part, Black Caribbean Christian youths reported greater sexual activity and types of sexual activity than African youth. Their sexual practices appeared more similar to the average Canadian youth.[28] Among Caribbean Christian males, 88.1 percent reported engagement in oral sex, whereas among Caribbean Christian females, the participation level was 70 percent. These figures exceeded those of African Christian males and females and Muslim youth.[29] Of course, one cannot fully discern the level of Christian commitment among these persons. It is likely their choice of the Christian label was somewhat nominal. At the same time, these numbers reflect religious trends in Black Christian youth from the Caribbean.

Articles concerning the place of the church among British-born, Caribbean youths suggest the waning influence of the church in the lives of these individuals.[30] This appears especially true among Caribbean youth from the first through the third generations. They do not frequent the Black churches and do not see it as their point of reference. They appear to question such things as the church's theology, priorities and the relevance to their own lives. Moreover, they desire a church that is responsive to their crises related to identity, social, economic and political needs.[31] Although there may be some trends in this direction in the USA, this author believes that religion continues to play a major role among Caribbean youth.

Although I am aware that trends in other Caribbean ethnic groups may not adequately reflect those among Black English-speaking people, one study may be worth noting. In this study, the author noted that Indo-Caribbean people tended to maintain their religious values. They

26. Archibald and Rhodd, "Measure of Acculturation for Afro-Caribbean Youth."

27. Maticka-Tyndale et al., "Profile of the Sexual Experiences."

28. Maticka-Tyndale et al., "Profile of the Sexual Experiences."

29. Maticka-Tyndale et al., "Profile of the Sexual Experiences."

30. Nathan, "African-Caribbean Youth Identity in the United Kingdom," 349.

31. Nathan, "African-Caribbean Youth Identity in the United Kingdom"; "Black Theology in Britain."

largely retained their Hindu or Muslim religion along with various other traditions,.[32] In this author's experience, the retaining of ancestral religions among Indo-Caribbeans exceeds the retaining of African-based religions among Afro-Caribbeans. However, in reference to Indo-Caribbeans, the authors noted that they did not retain other ethnic practices or even languages brought from India. In fact, only about 5 percent could even speak any Indian language.[33]

Cultural Traditions and Identity

In general, persons from the Caribbean, including youths, seem deeply connected to their Caribbean roots.[34] Although they are satisfied with immigration to the USA, they tend to idolize their home cultures. As a result, they resist assimilation to American culture choosing largely to hold onto their cultural identity and connections to their home countries.[35] Beyond this, Caribbean immigrants demonstrate a preference for things perceived as Caribbean rather than American. They tend to see choosing American cultural traditions as a neglect of Caribbean culture.[36] This strong connection and commitment to Caribbean culture and traditions is evident among first and second generation Black Caribbean persons and is especially true among second generation persons.[37] Although second generations person often lose their Caribbean accent and adopt American language, the commitment to the cultural traditions of the Caribbean remain strong.[38] However, there may be some regional differences in racial self-identification. One earlier study found that second generation children of Black Caribbean immigrants in the Miami area were more likely to assume a Black American identity than other second generation children.[39] The authors of this study noted that Black Caribbean children from lower socioeconomic classes largely influenced

32. Min, "Attachments of New York City Caribbean Indian Immigrants."

33. Min, "Attachments of New York City Caribbean Indian Immigrants."

34. Archibald and Rhodd, "Measure of Acculturation for Afro-Caribbean Youth"; Bridgewater and Buzzanell, "Caribbean Immigrants' Discourses"; Guy, "Black Immigrants of the Caribbean"; Sanchez, "Racial and Ego Identity Development."

35. Guy, "Black Immigrants of the Caribbean."

36. Archibald and Rhodd, "Measure of Acculturation for Afro-Caribbean Youth."

37. Sanchez, "Racial and Ego Identity Development."

38. Sanchez, "Racial and Ego Identity Development."

39. Thomas, "Socio-Demographic Determinants of Language Transition."

this pattern.[40] In other words, those Black Caribbean children from lower socioeconomic classes were much more likely to assume a Black American identity than those from higher socioeconomic classes.

Nevertheless, the general commitment to Caribbean culture appears to be a strong trend. The overall commitment to Caribbean culture often evidences itself in the concept of *citizenship transgression*.[41] This concept emerged from a study of Black immigrants mostly from the English-speaking Caribbean in the Phoenix, Arizona area. By this concept, the author referred to a reticence among interviewees to become naturalized citizens of the USA. They perceived such a move as almost a betrayal of their people and families. Instead, there was a tendency for the interviewees to desire to retain their country's passport.[42] This kind of data suggests the deep connections that these immigrants have to their originating countries and culture.

This commitment to the culture of their native lands influences how readily Black Caribbean immigrants, including adolescents, may identify with African Americans and their culture. Based on skin color, there is some initial identification with African Americans, yet they see themselves as different.[43] In fact, their ethnic identity as Caribbean people carries greater weight and significance than their racial identity as Black persons.[44] The mixture of identification with African Americans while at the same time remaining deeply committed to their native culture has been described as *cultural hybridity*.[45] Cultural hybridity involves the "complex mixture of identities that simultaneously connects and separates individuals from particular homogenous cultural groups."[46]

40. Thomas, "Socio-Demographic Determinants of Language Transition."

41. Wilson, "What It Means to Become a United States American."

42. Wilson, "What It Means to Become a United States American."

43. Archibald and Rhodd, "Measure of Acculturation for Afro-Caribbean Youth"; Guy, "Black Immigrants of the Caribbean"; Min, "Attachments of New York City Caribbean Indian Immigrants"; Sanchez, "Racial and Ego Identity Development"; Wheeler and Mahoney, "Caribbean Immigrants in the United States."

44. Sanchez, "Racial and Ego Identity Development."

45. Guy, "Black Immigrants of the Caribbean."

46. Guy, "Black Immigrants of the Caribbean," 20.

Cultural Race Related Stress and Engagement with African American Culture

Cultural race related stress may partly explain cultural hybridity and engagement with African American culture.[47] Race related stress is experienced through racism that expresses itself individually, institutionally and culturally.[48] Individually, much like African-Americans, Black people from the Caribbean are subjected to racial stereotypes and experience various prejudices that arise in an interpersonal context. They also experience racism through institutional policies and practices. Culturally, they encounter racism when their cultural values, beliefs and practices are deemed inferior to those of the majority culture.[49] How does this phenomenon explain the engagement of Black Caribbean with African-American culture? Black Caribbean immigrants are more likely to engage African-American culture when they perceive that Black persons are seen in a positive light and when they are not burdened by negative stereotypes. In contrast, when they perceive that their ethnic (Caribbean) group is seen positively, they are less likely to engage African-American culture. As a result, the authors of this study suggested that Black Caribbean immigrants engage African-American culture in largely functional ways depending on the perception of the favorability of their racial or ethnic group.[50]

Main Avenues of Migration to the USA

Reasons for Migration: Economics

Before speaking about the main avenues of migration to the USA, it seems reasonable to speak about the main reasons why people immigrate from the Caribbean to the USA. Of course, these reasons largely pertain to the adults who in turn bring their children with them or have them follow at a later date. Like many other persons who immigrate to the USA, English-speaking Black Caribbean immigrants migrate for economic, social and educational opportunities. They do so with the belief that these

---

47. Joseph et al., "Rules of Engagement."
48. Joseph et al., "Rules of Engagement."
49. Joseph et al., "Rules of Engagement."
50. Joseph et al., "Rules of Engagement."

opportunities will improve the lot of their children and families.[51] These immigrants often come motivated by idealistic thoughts about the American dream.[52] For example, in one study, the authors found that participants had seen and believed in the media's idealized depiction of America as a bountiful country providing opportunities for wealth and the easy life.[53] This idealized image of America provided prime motivation for immigration to this country. Strangely enough, the authors also noted that these immigrants perpetuated this mythic view of America when they returned to their respective countries.[54]

Given this idealized image of America as a land of plenty, it's evident that economic interests serve as the major motivating factor and exert the foremost influence for immigration to the United States; immigrants migrate to work hoping that this will allow them to improve their economic lot.[55] This economic motivation serves as the primary basis for immigration even when immigrants ostensibly appear to have migrated for educational reasons. In such cases, the economic reason is nearly always in the background providing the major impetus.[56] This does not mean one should ignore the educational goals that spur these individuals to immigrate. However, these immigrants often perceive education as a springboard for achieving career goals that will ultimately permit them to advance financially. In short, Caribbean immigrants see education as the means to achievement and gaining economic stability for themselves and their families.[57]

51. Archibald and Rhodd, "Measure of Acculturation for Afro-Caribbean Youth"; Bridgewater and Buzzanell, "Caribbean Immigrants' Discourses"; Jackson et al., "Use of Mental Health Services"; Murphy and Mahalingam, "Perceived Congruence between Expectations and Outcomes."

52. Bridgewater and Buzzanell, "Caribbean Immigrants' Discourses."

53. Bridgewater and Buzzanell, "Caribbean Immigrants' Discourses."

54. Bridgewater and Buzzanell, "Caribbean Immigrants' Discourses."

55. Bridgewater and Buzzanell, "Caribbean Immigrants' Discourses"; Guy, "Black Immigrants of the Caribbean"; Jackson et al., "Use of Mental Health Services"; Murphy and Mahalingam, "Perceived Congruence between Expectations and Outcomes"; Smith et al., "Serial Migration and Its Implications for the Parent-Child Relationship"; Wheeler and Mahoney, "Caribbean Immigrants in the United States."

56. Bridgewater and Buzzanell, "Caribbean Immigrants' Discourses"; Jackson et al., "Use of Mental Health Services"; Murphy and Mahalingam, "Perceived Congruence between Expectations and Outcomes."

57. Bridgewater and Buzzanell, "Caribbean Immigrants' Discourses"; Jackson et al., "Use of Mental Health Services."

Family Filing of Immigration Papers

Having set these reasons as a backdrop for the immigration of Black Caribbean Immigrants to the USA, we can proceed to discuss the main avenues of immigration. Of course, as is true in other immigrant groups, some live in the country illegally. They might have come for a visit or for educational purposes and remained past the allotted period of time. Of course, these avenues largely apply to adults and not children or adolescents. However, many immigrate legally. They do so through the filing of immigration papers by their relatives already in the USA. Given this reality, family members play a significant role in the migration patterns of Black Caribbean immigrants.[58] Indeed, Black immigrants from the Caribbean are likely to demonstrate a great deal of contact with family members.[59] In addition to facilitating the filing of papers for family members, immediate and extended family members play other significant roles that enable the immigration of their loved ones. Family members might perform such instrumental roles as assisting or providing the financial support that permits immigration of their loved ones. Beyond this, family members back in the homeland also provide assistance by caring for the children of the parent(s) who immigrated. Moreover, family members already in the USA might assist the new immigrant through various efforts to help them settle and gain employment.[60]

Serial Migration

The major role that family plays in the migration of Black immigrants from the Caribbean relates closely to a unique immigration pattern evident in this group. *Serial migration* is the name given to this migration pattern.[61]

58. Jackson et al., "Use of Mental Health Services"; Jackson et al., "Age Cohort, Ancestry, and Immigrant Generation Influences."

59. Jackson et al., "Use of Mental Health Services"; Murphy and Mahalingam, "Perceived Congruence between Expectations and Outcomes"; Smith et al., "Serial Migration and Its Implications for the Parent-Child Relationship."

60. Jackson et al., "Use of Mental Health Services"; Jackson et al., "Age Cohort, Ancestry, and Immigrant Generation Influences"; Murphy and Mahalingam, "Perceived Congruence between Expectations and Outcomes."

61. Murphy and Mahalingam, "Perceived Congruence between Expectations and Outcomes"; Roopnarine et al., "Beliefs about Mothers' and Fathers' Roles"; Smith et al., "Serial Migration and Its Implications for the Parent-Child Relationship"; Wheeler and Mahoney, "Caribbean Immigrants in the United States."

It is generally seen as an adaptive response adopted by immigrants from the Caribbean. This pattern equips immigrants with the ability to handle the uncertainty, attending insecurity and financial costs associated with migration to a new country.[62]

Serial migration occurs when one or both parents immigrate to the USA for employment purposes. In so doing, they often blaze a path in which the rest of their family will follow at a later date.[63] The pattern occurs in at least two stages: First, there is the initial separation of the immigrating parent(s) from their children. Second, this initial separation is followed by the eventual reuniting of the family.[64] Typically, if only one parental figure immigrates it is usually the woman in the family. As a result, women tend to dominate during the first phase of the serial migration pattern. Once they shift to an immigration status that permits them to bring their family to the USA, their spouses and children eventually follow.[65] However, the eventual migration of their children and the reunion of the family often takes a number of years to come to fruition.[66] The long periods of separation from nuclear family members often create problems for the family at a later date. This pattern often creates major adjustment problems for children.[67]

Success Factors of Black Caribbean Immigrants

Although it would be easy to move directly to addressing some of the challenges English-speaking Black immigrants face, I have chosen a somewhat different approach. As a result, I will focus on some of the successes and the factors that contribute to this success among this immigrant group.

62. Smith et al., "Serial Migration and Its Implications for the Parent-Child Relationship."

63. Murphy and Mahalingam, "Perceived Congruence between Expectations and Outcomes"; Smith et al., "Serial Migration and Its Implications for the Parent-Child Relationship"; Wheeler and Mahoney, "Caribbean Immigrants in the United States."

64. Smith et al., "Serial Migration and Its Implications for the Parent-Child Relationship."

65. Smith et al., "Serial Migration and Its Implications for the Parent-Child Relationship."

66. Murphy and Mahalingam, "Perceived Congruence between Expectations and Outcomes"; Smith et al., "Serial Migration and Its Implications for the Parent-Child Relationship"; Wheeler and Mahoney, "Caribbean Immigrants in the United States."

67. Smith et al., "Serial Migration and Its Implications for the Parent-Child Relationship"; Wheeler and Mahoney, "Caribbean Immigrants in the United States."

Socialized as Majority Persons

What are some of the successes among this group and how does one explain these? One major factor in the success of these immigrants focuses on their positive socialization process.[68] However, not everyone agrees with this thesis that attributes some advantage to growing up in a favorable environment where these persons were the racial majority.[69] Nevertheless, various authors highlight this favorable environment as a definite asset.[70] Accordingly, they believe the socialization in a positive atmosphere helped to forge a resilient and positive identity in these individuals. Their psychological makeup also benefited from a history within their countries that provided opportunities for personal and financial success.[71] Furthermore, this positive environment served to develop persons with an inherently good work ethic and a drive to pursue achievement.[72] Other authors expressed a similar sentiment.[73] For example, some pointed to Black English-speaking Caribbean immigrants as persons who were conditioned to seize the opportunities presented to them and to thrive within the USA; they not only adjusted and persevered in their new environment but in many ways demonstrated a work ethic that exceeded that of the USA.[74]

One finds these traits described in the following quotation taken from an article that interviewed a number of persons from the English-speaking Caribbean: "In these stories, participants expressed their beliefs that West Indian cultural discourses told a moral tale of Caribbean people as being resourceful, successful, and adaptable. They maintained that they were successful in their new environment because they were taught from an early age to seize challenges but do so in the Caribbean way."[75] Given this kind of socialization, Black Caribbean persons are likely to reject the idea of *minority-ness*. While accepting that they are perceived as minorities and are

68. Corra and Kimuna, "Double Jeopardy?"; Fournillier and Lewis, "Finding Voice"; Kalmijn, "Socioeconomic Assimilation of Caribbean American Blacks."

69. Model, *West Indian Immigrants.*

70. Corra and Kimuna, "Double Jeopardy?"; Fournillier and Lewis, "Finding Voice"; Kalmijn, "Socioeconomic Assimilation of Caribbean American Blacks."

71. Corra and Kimuna, "Double Jeopardy?"

72. Corra and Kimuna, "Double Jeopardy?"

73. Bridgewater and Buzzanell, "Caribbean Immigrants' Discourses"; Fournillier and Lewis, "Finding Voice."

74. Bridgewater and Buzzanell, "Caribbean Immigrants' Discourses."

75. Bridgewater and Buzzanell, "Caribbean Immigrants' Discourses."

in fact a minority in the USA, they still hold to the majority environment and perspectives that shaped their being.[76]

Positive Socialization in Black Caribbean Immigrant Children

Obviously, not all of these realities will pertain to the children of Black Caribbean immigrants. How well they become socialized in this positive identity and how it impacts their identity and acculturation will depend on various factors. For example, it partly depends on how well parents are able to inculcate into their children the positive socialization process and their prior identity as racial majorities into their children. It also partly depends on the age when they migrated. Significantly, it has been found that those who immigrated as young adults, ages eighteen to thirty-four, seemed to possess some protection against developing mental disorders.[77] Evidently then, those children who migrated to the USA in their later teens are more likely to have developed the kind of resilient psyche that can withstand some of the difficulties of the acculturation process.[78] On the other side, those children born to Black Caribbean immigrants may be somewhat at risk. This is linked to the fact that USA-born Caribbean Blacks tend to show higher rates of mental disorders that those who immigrated to this country.[79]

Family and Support

One might point to other areas that likely play a role in the success of immigrant groups from the Caribbean area. Persons from the Caribbean in all age groups exhibit frequent contact with family members and report emotional closeness with relatives. This remains true regardless of distance or age.[80]

We have already seen the instrumental support that family members in the USA provide; they often open doors to employment and otherwise help the immigrants to settle into the country. Likewise, family members back in the Caribbean also provide instrumental and other support

76. Fournillier and Lewis, "Finding Voice."

77. Williams et al., "Mental Health of Black Caribbean Immigrants."

78. Williams et al., "Mental Health of Black Caribbean Immigrants."

79. Williams et al., "Mental Health of Black Caribbean Immigrants."

80. Jackson et al., "Use of Mental Health Services"; Jackson et al., "Age Cohort, Ancestry and Immigrant Generation."

that facilitates immigration.[81] This sort of support appears more critical to women than men and is necessary for the survival of their families. Women tend to depend more on this kind of social support as it plays a key factor in the well-being of their children.[82] This close contact with family both in the USA and Caribbean doubtless contributes to their success. But family support also contributes to the success of adolescents; they are more able to shake off the adjustment impact of family stresses through support from family networks.[83]

Support from the Caribbean Community

But family members are not the only persons with whom English-speaking Caribbean immigrants form a communal bond that support their success as immigrants; they also form bonds with other English-speaking immigrants who come from different islands than themselves. They develop what was described as *West Indian nationalism*.[84] Connections to the wider Caribbean community might take place through several avenues including connections in the workplace, rotating credit associations, Caribbean festivals and even through sports association, especially revolving around cricket. These types of associations serve to recreate various aspects of the culture to which they were accustomed.[85] These cultural connections especially when it comes to the sport of Cricket does not simply apply to Black Caribbean immigrants. It also applies to Indo-Caribbean immigrants. They exhibit greater allegiance to the Caribbean than to India. Thus, in a hypothetical cricket match, Indo-Caribbeans would to a large degree cheer for their island team rather than India.[86] Indeed, from this author's experience, the regional West Indies cricket team garners major support from all English-speaking Caribbean people, regardless of race.

This attachment to other English-speaking immigrants seems to serve several purposes: First, such community contact provides a measure of security that stimulates exploration, work and contributions in their new

81. Jackson et al., "Use of Mental Health Services"; Murphy and Mahalingam, "Perceived Congruence Between Expectations and Outcomes."

82. Lorick-Wilmot, *Creating Black Ethnic Identity*.

83. Goosby et al., "Ethnic Differences."

84. Regis, "Theoretical Framework."

85. Regis, "Theoretical Framework."

86. Min, "Attachments of New York City Caribbean Indian Immigrants."

country. Second, such communities also provide a place of safety and re-treat during difficult times.[87] Beyond these, connections with other persons from the English-speaking Caribbean seems to provide an immediate and present substitute for their homelands. The connections also appear to pro-vide an impetus for achievement in their new home.[88]

Successes

Having spoken about some of the factors that play a role in their success, it is now appropriate to briefly highlight a few of these successes. Overall, English-speaking Caribbean immigrants generally fare better than other groups from the Caribbean.[89] First, this group exhibits a high level of education attainment when compared to African Americans.[90] One sees this among persons in the eighteen to fifty-four age group and it is especially pronounced among Black immigrants from the English-speaking Caribbean.[91] For example, in 2000, 25.7 percent of Black immigrants from the English-speaking Caribbean held a college degree whereas the rate among African Americans during the same period was 20.6 percent.[92] They also tend to fare better financially than persons from the Spanish and French Caribbean islands. In fact, when one compares immigrants from African, English, French and Spanish-speaking immigrants, the English-speaking Caribbean immigrants fare better than the other groups. Moreover, those from the Spanish and French speaking islands were the lowest among these four groups.[93]

Besides the advantage in educational attainment, these immigrants also experience a measure of economic and financial success. Their in-come tends to exceed that of African Americans as well as immigrants from French and Spanish Caribbean countries.[94] Moreover, in general,

87. Regis, "Theoretical Framework."

88. Regis, "Theoretical Framework."

89. Joseph et al., "Rules of Engagement"; Kalmijn, "Socioeconomic Assimilation of Caribbean American Blacks."

90. Jackson et al., "Use of Mental Health Services"; Joseph et al., "Rules of Engage-ment"; Kalmijn, "Socioeconomic Assimilation of Caribbean American Blacks."

91. Jackson et al., "Use of Mental Health Services."

92. Jackson et al., "Use of Mental Health Services."

93. Kalmijn, "Socioeconomic Assimilation of Caribbean American Blacks."

94. Corra and Kimuna, "Double Jeopardy?"; Jackson et al., "Use of Mental Health Services"; Kalmijn, "Socioeconomic Assimilation"; Model et al., "Black Caribbeans in Comparative Perspective."

persons from the English-speaking Caribbean attract better wages than the groups identified above. This generally holds true whether they possess a college degree or not.[95]

Unique Challenges of Navigating the USA Culture

Economic Barriers

Of course, Black immigrants from the English-speaking Caribbean also face a number of unique challenges. Even though these immigrants generally fare better financially than other immigrant groups from the Caribbean, problems still exist. Much of this derives from their racial status which limits the resources and opportunities made available to them.[96] Limited opportunities, especially in terms of employment, is especially true among Caribbean males. They normally experience greater economic problems than their female counterparts. As a rule, Caribbean males experience more hurdles in the job market than Caribbean females. As a result, they tend to experience high rates of unemployment.[97] The challenges are especially difficult for adolescents seeking employment. One author lamented this plight of youth in the following words: "There is an increasing number of youth living in cities in the developing world that are facing daunting economic and social challenges, including social exclusion, lack of economic opportunities, and limited access to resources. They are increasingly marginalized, excluded from the economic growth of cities, and forced to live on the margins of society."[98] Although this comment was made in reference to youth living in cities in the developing world, this reality also applies to youth in the USA. For example, in July 2013, the unemployment rate among those between eighteen and twenty-nine stood at 16.1 percent. This rate represented the highest sustained unemployment rate since World War II.[99] This evidently represented the rate among male adolescents since

95. Corra and Kimuna, "Double Jeopardy?"

96. Guy, "Black Immigrants of the Caribbean"; Kalmijn, "Socioeconomic Assimilation."

97. Corra and Kimuna, "Black Immigrants of the Caribbean"; Model et al., "Black Caribbeans in Comparative Perspective"; Wheeler and Mahoney, "Caribbean Immigrants in the US."

98. Ali, "Youth Unemployment," 14.

99. Carmona, "US Youth Employment."

the rate for women of the same age range stood at 10.8 percent.[100] The figure is even higher among those of African descent; African Americans in the same age bracket had a rate of 20.9 percent.[101] One would expect a similar rate among Black Caribbean immigrants. Given this kind of data, the plight of adolescents and young adults is a dire one.

Health Barriers

Health is another area that presents challenges to the Black Caribbean immigrant. A substantial number of Caribbean immigrants experience declining physical and emotional health.[102] Much of this can be attributed to factors within the society, including racism, that serve to limit access to necessary health services.[103] Additionally, it's hypothesized that the needs within this group are not well understood.[104] Some of these immigrants, especially undocumented immigrants, lack basic health insurance and may also hold to beliefs and practices regarding health that further compromise them in this area.[105] Additionally, those without legal immigration status face major obstacles to accessing the health care system. They may live in urban communities with poor conditions that expose them to higher rates of HIV and sexually transmitted diseases.[106] They also often work under difficult conditions that further exacerbate declines in health.[107] Moreover, members within this community can become vulnerable to certain risky behaviors that further serve to compromise their health status.[108] Most vulnerable to these high risk behaviors are those undocumented Caribbean immigrants. Because of a lack of resources, they often live in inferior living conditions with high incidences of sexually transmitted diseases and HIV.[109]

100. Carmona, "US Youth Employment."

101. Carmona, "US Youth Employment."

102. Wheeler and Mahoney, "Caribbean Immigrants in the US."

103. Wheeler and Mahoney, "Caribbean Immigrants in the US"; Williams et al., "Mental Health of Black Caribbean Immigrants."

104. Wheeler and Mahoney, "Caribbean Immigrants in the US."

105. Wheeler and Mahoney, "Caribbean Immigrants in the US."

106. Archibald and Rhodd, "Measure of Acculturation for Afro-Caribbean Youth."

107. Archibald and Rhodd, "Measure of Acculturation for Afro-Caribbean Youth"; Wheeler and Mahoney, "Caribbean Immigrants in the US."

108. Archibald and Rhodd, "Measure of Acculturation for Afro-Caribbean Youth."

109. Archibald and Rhodd, "Measure of Acculturation for Afro-Caribbean Youth."

Risky Behaviors in Adolescents

Documented and undocumented adolescents also more easily succumb to risky health-related behaviors. These risky behaviors tend to characterize those in lower socioeconomic brackets. Adolescents and young Caribbean adults often adopt these behaviors as a way of identifying with those who hold a lower socioeconomic status.[110] They often prefer to adopt these behaviors rather than be ridiculed as foreigners. Indeed, whether legal or illegal, adolescents are most prone to engage in the risky behaviors present within their communities.[111]

Unfortunately, some of the risky practices adopted by young immigrants in the Black Caribbean community relate to sexuality. Such persons tend to identify with the overall sexual practices of the community to which they immigrate.[112] As cited earlier, this was documented in a Canadian study of the sexual practices of Black Caribbean immigrant youths. For example, ¾ of the Black Caribbean youth reported sexual experiences primarily in the area of penile vaginal intercourse and oral sex although they also engaged in masturbation and fingering.[113] Among African immigrant youth, the percentage was less than half.[114] Additionally, the Black Caribbean immigrant youths reported greater sexual experiences including a greater number of sexual partners. They also tended to initiate sexual experiences at a younger age.[115] Although this recent research comes from Canada, given its location in North America and similarities between Canada and the US, it's likely the results might generalize here to some degree. As in Canada, it's also likely that Black Caribbean immigrant adolescents may be at greater risk for sexual behaviors that may expose them to HIV and STDs. This is especially true of males within this population as they demonstrate more sexual experimentation than females in the same group.[116]

110. Archibald and Rhodd, "Measure of Acculturation for Afro-Caribbean Youth"; Thomas, "Socio-Demographic Determinants."

111. Archibald and Rhodd, "Measure of Acculturation for Afro-Caribbean Youth."

112. Archibald and Rhodd, "Measure of Acculturation for Afro-Caribbean Youth"; Maticka-Tyndale et al., "Profile of the Sexual Experiences."

113. Maticka-Tyndale et al., "Profile of the Sexual Experiences."

114. Maticka-Tyndale et al., "Profile of the Sexual Experiences."

115. Maticka-Tyndale et al., "Profile of the Sexual Experiences."

116. Maticka-Tyndale et al., "Profile of the Sexual Experiences."

Mental Health Challenges

Besides physical risks that compromise health, one can also point to challenges related to the mental health of Black Caribbean immigrants. However, at the outset it should be noted that there is a great degree of variation in mental health within this population.[117] The mental health of these immigrants can vary by a number of characteristics. The characteristics can include elements such as language, age at immigration, being born outside of the USA, length of residence in the USA and generational status.[118] For example, at least one study has documented that the length of time lived within the USA is linked to the increased risk for various mental illnesses.[119] Similarly, those born in the USA generally exhibit higher rates of mental disorders. This reality relates to their lack of experience in being a racial majority which seems to provide protective factors against mental problems.[120] Significantly, those who immigrated between eighteen and thirty-four seem to possess the greatest insulation against mental disorders.[121]

There also appears to be a stigma attached to the use of mental health services among Caribbean immigrants. Such concerns play a major role in preventing the depressed in these groups from seeking mental health services.[122] Lower socio-economic status also appears to play a role in the underutilization of mental health services. Low utilization rates especially apply to those adolescents between thirteen and seventeen and those older than thirty-six.[123] Age also appears related to the use of mental health services. Thus, pre-teens who immigrated to the USA before age twelve were much more likely to utilize mental health services even when they did not have a mental disorder.[124] Similarly, among those who possessed a mental disorder, adolescents between the ages of thirteen to seventeen and thirty-five plus at the time of their immigration, used mental health services at a much higher rate that those younger than twelve or between eighteen and thirty-four.[125]

117. Williams et al., "Mental Health of Black Caribbean Immigrants."

118. Jackson et al., "Use of Mental Health Services"; Williams et al., "Mental Health of Black Caribbean Immigrants."

119. Williams et al., "Mental Health of Black Caribbean Immigrants."

120. Williams et al., "Mental Health of Black Caribbean Immigrants."

121. Williams et al., "Mental Health of Black Caribbean Immigrants."

122. Wheeler and Mahoney, "Mental Health of Black Caribbean Immigrants."

123. Shervin and Caldwell, "Neighborhood Safety and Major Depressive Disorder."

124. Jackson et al., "Use of Mental Health Services."

125. Jackson et al., "Use of Mental Health Services."

Given these findings, it's likely that "socialization and access to mental health services play an important role in use of those services."[126]

Having said this, one can draw other general conclusions relative to mental health. For example, mental disorders such as depression and anxiety have been documented in this population.[127] In general, Caribbean men tend to exhibit higher rates of these problems and lifetime psychological disorders than African Americans.[128] This reality likely points to greater difficulties in cultural adjustment among Black Caribbean males.[129] In contrast, the rates among women tend to be lower.[130] In comparison to their African American counterparts, Caribbean women tend to show lower rates of anxiety and substance related disorders. In fact, compared to this group, they show up lower on any mental disorder.[131] This same pattern is likely to exist among adolescents within the English-speaking Black Caribbean community.

Perceived Discrimination and Mental Challenges

Perceived discrimination likely contributes to the mental health problems among Black Caribbean youths. Among adolescents sixteen years or older, perceived discrimination contributes to increases in symptoms of depression while also contributing to lowered self-esteem and life satisfaction.[132] Perceived discrimination also explains some of the gender differences in mental health. For example, 90 percent of Black Caribbean youth report at least one act of discrimination within a year and they exhibit greater vulnerability to psychological disorders when they experience high levels of

---

126. Jackson et al., "Use of Mental Health Services," 64.

127. Murphy and Mahalingam, "Perceived Congruence Between Expectations and Outcomes"; Wheeler and Mahoney, "Caribbean Immigrants in the United States."

128. Shervin and Caldwell, "Neighborhood Safety and Major Depressive Disorder"; Taylor et al.,"Comorbid Mood and Anxiety Disorders"; Williams et al., "Mental Health of Black Caribbean Immigrants."

129. Shervin and Caldwell, "Neighborhood Safety and Major Depressive Disorder"; Taylor et al.,"Comorbid Mood and Anxiety Disorders."

130. Shervin and Caldwell, "Neighborhood Safety and Major Depressive Disorder"; Taylor et al.,"Comorbid Mood and Anxiety Disorders"; Williams et al., "Mental Health of Black Caribbean Immigrants."

131. Williams et al., "Mental Health of Black Caribbean Immigrants."

132. Seaton et al., "Intersectional Approach for Understanding Perceived Discrimination."

discrimination.[133] This perceived discrimination generally appears to be more harmful to Black Caribbean youth than African American youth.[134] However, there are also age and gender differences. For example, adolescents in the later stages perceive more discrimination and experience more decreases in life satisfaction and self-esteem than those in the early or middle stages of adolescence.[135] Additionally, Black male youths most often experience more discrimination than Black females.[136] Although these experiences contribute to lower satisfactions levels, they do not appear to impact the psychological well-being of Black Caribbean males. This particular finding appears contrary to other studies that usually find an overall negative impact from discrimination.[137] Surprisingly, although perceived discrimination did not appear to impact the psychological well-being of Black Caribbean males, it negatively impacted the emotional health of Black Caribbean females. Influenced by perceived discrimination, they reported higher levels of depression coupled with lowered self-esteem and life satisfaction. They also tended to engage in more risky behaviors.[138] The authors hypothesized that these negative repercussions came about because of their tendency to ruminate more about the perceived discrimination.[139]

Unsafe Neighborhoods and Mental Challenges

While addressing perception related issues, it seems appropriate to address the views of Black Caribbean Youths regarding the safety of their neighborhoods and how this impacts mental health. Due to widespread exposure to violence, Black youth experience fears relative to the safety of their neighborhoods. In turn, such fears relate to declines in physical and mental health among black youth. In particular, such fears often contribute to a major risk

133. Seaton et al., "Prevalence of Perceived Discrimination."

134. Seaton et al., "Prevalence of Perceived Discrimination."

135. Seaton et al., "Prevalence of Perceived Discrimination"; "Intersectional Approach for Understanding Perceived Discrimination."

136. Seaton et al., "Prevalence of Perceived Discrimination"; "Intersectional Approach for Understanding Perceived Discrimination."

137. Seaton et al., "Prevalence of Perceived Discrimination"; "Intersectional Approach for Understanding Perceived Discrimination."

138. Seaton et al., "Intersectional Approach for Understanding Perceived Discrimination."

139. Seaton et al., "Intersectional Approach for Understanding Perceived Discrimination."

for depression.[140] Surprisingly, in one study, these perceptions regarding one's neighborhood was not related to a higher incidence of major depression disorder in either Black Caribbean males and females.[141] However, even though there was no decline in mental health, the study found that more Black Caribbean females than males saw their neighborhoods as unsafe.[142]

Effects of Challenges on General Life in the USA

In this section I will principally focus on the impact of immigration on families and their children and the implications for family conflict. Earlier I noted the serial migration pattern that is especially true among Black Caribbean immigrants. Although this pattern carries some advantages in terms of communal support, the separation and reuniting of families can cause major problems. In fact, it often brings such families into contact with the mental health system.[143] In such encounters, a number of issues come to the surface. They include "issues of loyalty, identity development, discipline and authority, isolation, rejection and counter rejection, estrangement, abandonment, disillusionment, and bereavement."[144]

Obviously, this pattern also creates significant difficulties for families and how they relate to their children. Given the long periods of separation that sometimes attend the serial migration pattern, rifts can appear in the bonds between family members and especially between parents and children. Moreover, the passing of time does not effectively repair the rifts between parents and children.[145] The length of the separation can also create deep bonds with the caregivers so much so that they come to see the caregivers as their parents. This often negatively impacts reunion with their biological parents.[146] In addition, children can experience a sense of abandonment and the feelings that attend such an experience.[147] Moreover, the serial migration pattern can also contribute to self-esteem and behavioral

140. Shervin and Caldwell, "Neighborhood Safety and Major Depressive Disorder."

141. Shervin and Caldwell, "Neighborhood Safety and Major Depressive Disorder."

142. Shervin and Caldwell, "Neighborhood Safety and Major Depressive Disorder."

143. Smith et al., "Serial Migration and Its Implications."

144. Smith et al., "Serial Migration and Its Implications," 110.

145. Smith et al., "Serial Migration and Its Implications."

146. Smith et al., "Serial Migration and Its Implications."

147. Smith et al., "Serial Migration and Its Implications"; Wheeler and Mahoney, "Caribbean Immigrants in the United States."

problems in children.[148] Of course, not all families experience this kind of pain. However, for other families, the reuniting of family members can create a great deal of turmoil.[149]

Immigration and its attending processes also demands a number of adjustments from all parties concerned, including children and adolescents. Children and adolescents often encounter issues revolving around their adjustment to a new country. This adjustment proves far more difficult for those children who were left behind when parents immigrated.[150] One might encounter problems such as depression, anger or anxiety in such children. They may also act out through involvement with delinquent behavior.[151] In contrast, it is far easier for those who initially immigrated along with their parents.[152]

Family Stress and Adolescent Appraisals

While discussing the topic of adjustment, it's important to speak about the stress generated in families as they seek to adjust to a new culture. Needless to say, immigration and its associated processes generate a significant amount of stress within families.[153] In turn, stress within families can lead adolescents to make more stress appraisals. However, surprisingly, in one study, the increase in parental stressors correlated with better adolescent adjustment. Additionally, parental stressors bore no relationship to depressive symptomology in the same adolescents.[154] The authors hypothesized that this unexpected finding was likely due to the adolescents' possession and use of extended family networks.[155] Significantly, in Black Caribbean communities, those persons who are younger and older receive the greatest amount of family support.[156] This augurs well for children and adolescents in these communities

148. Smith et al., "Serial Migration and Its Implications."

149. Smith et al., "Serial Migration and Its Implications."

150. Smith et al., "Serial Migration and Its Implications."

151. Smith et al., "Serial Migration and Its Implications."

152. Smith et al., "Serial Migration and Its Implications."

153. Goosby et al., "Ethnic Differences in Family Stress Processes."

154. Goosby et al., "Ethnic Differences in Family Stress Processes."

155. Goosby et al., "Ethnic Differences in Family Stress Processes."

156. Goosby et al., "Ethnic Differences in Family Stress Processes."

Conclusion

In this chapter, I have tried to paint an overall picture of the Black English-speaking Caribbean immigrant while placing some emphasis on the experiences of children and adolescents in this immigrant group. The picture is somewhat mixed. Black Caribbean adolescents face a number of challenges. The serial migration pattern that characterizes Black Caribbean immigrants poses a major difficulty for children and their parents as they reunite.[157] It can cause a number of family conflicts and difficulties that threaten to break apart the family.

One can also speak about the racial stereotypes applied to persons of color, particularly those of African descent, that are ascribed to Black Caribbean immigrants. Because of such racial attitudes and practices, these immigrants, including adolescents, face a number of hurdles such as perceived discrimination, unemployment, physical and mental health problems.[158] These difficulties can foster the adoption of risky behaviors. Black Caribbean adolescent males seem especially at risk as they face more perceived discrimination, stereotypic labels and greater unemployment. This does not mean that Black adolescent females escape without any negative impact. For example, the perception of discrimination appears to have greater negative impact on females than males. Black Caribbean adolescent females also appear to be more negatively impacted by the lack of safety within their neighborhoods.[159]

However, within these immigrant communities, there exists factors that contribute to their success and that of their children. For example, these immigrants come from communities in which they were racial majorities and they often bring this mentality with them.[160] If they can inculcate aspects of this resilience within their children, it augurs well for their success. These immigrants also experience a great degree of support

157. Murphy and Mahalingam, "Perceived Congruence Between Expectations and Outcomes"; Smith et al., "Serial Migration and Its Implications"; Wheeler and Mahoney, "Caribbean Immigrants in the United States."

158. Carmona, "US Youth Employment"; Jackson et al., "Use of Mental Health Services"; Jackson et al., "Age Cohort, Ancestry, and Immigrant Generational Influences"; Seaton et al., "Prevalence of Perceived Discrimination"; "Intersectional Approach for Understanding Perceived Discrimination"; Williams et al., "Mental Health of Black Caribbean Immigrants."

159. Shervin and Caldwell, "Neighborhood Safety and Major Depressive Disorder."

160. Corra and Kimuna, "Double Jeopardy?"; Fournillier and Lewis, "Finding Voice"; Kalmijn, "Socioeconomic Assimilation of Caribbean American Blacks."

within their families in the USA and in their native countries as well as from the community of Caribbean in their locales. This kind of support appears especially critical to younger and older immigrants as they deal with the pressures associated with living in a different country.[161]

161. Goosby et al., "Ethnic Differences in Family Stress Processes."

III

Intervention Models

8

"It Takes A Village" (ITAV) Camps

Possibilities for Developing Rites of Passage for Immigrants

—Chris Kiesling and Anne Kiome Gatobu

When I (Chris) first stepped into the role of professor at Asbury Seminary two decades ago I inherited from my predecessor, Dr. Donald Joy, a backpacking/trailcamp class that he had been directing for more than ten years. The curriculum for the class was built around a rite of passage model detailed in Victor Turner's work. Dr. Joy had become increasingly concerned about Western culture's tendency to keep teens in a place of perpetual adolescence rather than guiding them toward adult responsibilities. He recognized that rites of initiation practiced throughout the world could resource Christian communities as they considered their own means of developing youth into adults who were living into a faith of their own.[1]

This chapter offers an overview of the model used in conceptualizing rites of initiation by introducing various aspects of the rites as they are practiced around the world. It then describes ways the model was practiced via backpacking/trail camp trips. Throughout the chapter we suggest ways that we believe different immigrant groups might utilize this material. Our hope is that we could stimulate conversation toward an eventual collective body of research, experimentation, reflective thought and derived wisdom that could help a variety of ethnic groups sponsor younger generations into adulthood.

Given the tendency toward family dissonance during developmental junctures, we wondered whether carefully constructed rites of passage might have the power to help teens and parents integrate their words

1. Joy, *Empower Your Kids to Be Adults.*

amicably and with clearer expectations. These are the stages where the differing cultures of the first generation immigrant parents and that of their children growing in the West are most pronounced. Hence, rites of passage could be intentionally utilized to bridge the cultural gaps and create safe spaces that lead to amicable relationships. They are therefore the focus of this chapter.

The African idiom *"it takes a village to raise a child "* invites adaptation for any of the ethnic groups or varied programs. We use the term " It Takes a Village" (ITAV) to point to the general idea that effective rites require the input of a relational system beyond the immediate parents that would create formative space that honors both the uniqueness of children and the competing cultural dynamics in which they are being socialized. ITAV camps should therefore not be regarded as overly prescriptive but rather suggestive of a generally loose model that can be adapted in various ways to honor the values, morals and traditions of any particular group of people. Important characteristics of an ITAV camp model that are essential to any adtptation include: the presence of active faith in the majority of the sponsors; the involvement of extended family and friends of participating family in the orchestration of the camp, and the utilization of rituals that are meaningful to the families involved.

Also, we acknowledges that first generation immigrant children may at first approach these rites with mistrust. Given the treatment they may have received at school or elsewhere as non-fitting Americans, enacting a ritual that reinforces cultural heritage may be resisted. They may question the judgement of parents to involve them, and perhaps their peers, in a ceremony that is not standard in majority culture or required of their fellow Caucasian friends. Careful use of a *"village'* to design the camp, may serve to counteract some of this skepticism. Targeted friends and family of the families may be invited to be part of the planning. Mentors may be chosen from within and without the cultural circle so as to balance perspective. To allow the feel of a true village, families that know each other well, have some history together, and share a common faith, can create familiarity in designing the experience together. Basic training in listening and coaching may also enhance the effectiveness of mentors, spurring teenagers on without the rite becoming a proscriptive lecture.

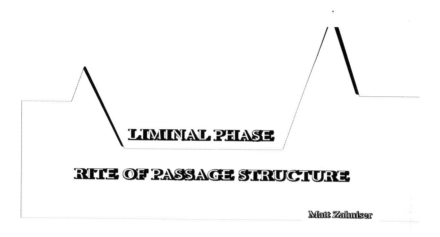

The pictorial above attempts to capture the universal and structural aspects of a rite of passage.[2] Van Gennep was among the first to write about such rites, conceptualizing them as an individual moving between separate groupings of a society.[3] Hence a "passage" quite literally conveyed the changing of rooms and/or the movement from one group to another. This broad characterization allows for wide application of the model. Jewish children at the age of thirteen move from being under the authority of their parents to a place of accountability. Bar or Bat mitzvah literally conveying that they are now "sons or daughters of the commandments" and subject to the law. Latin American cultures often promote a fifteen-year-old girl from childhood to womanhood with a quinceanera. Some Native American cultures practiced a vision quest entailing sending young boys into a sacred space in a natural setting where they would pray and cry out to the spirits that they might have a vision that helps them know their purpose in life, role in their community and ways to serve their people. Circumcision is practiced in rites of passage ceremonies in Africa that quite literally mark a boy's admittance into adulthood. Certain sects of the Amish practice Rumspringa, permitting teenaged youth the chance to "run around," gaining some knowledge of the outside world, before deciding to be baptized into the community or to leave it altogether. Other groups practice ritualized actions to signify movement between groups such as debutante balls that set young women of upper class society on "debut" for eligible bachelors. Other rites include hooding

2. Zahniser and Whiteman, *Symbol and Ceremony.*
3. Van Gennep, *"Les rites de passage."*

or graduation ceremonies in educational settings, first menstruation, first communion preceded by first confession in Catholic tradition, confirmation, sweet sixteen birthday parties, scarification/tattooing/body piercing, getting a driver's license or giving away one's virginity.[4]

Some years ago, I (Chris) came across a National Public Radio broadcast citing a study by a Sports Illustrated columnist Gregory Warner, who was exploring what made Kenyan runners the winners in so many marathons. That year Wilson Kipsang, a Kenyan, set a new record for the Berlin Marathon. Fellow Kenyans also placed second, third, fourth, and fifth place. On the women's side, Kenyans placed first, second, fourth. Two weeks later in Chicago, Dennis Kimetto broke that marathon course record and three more Kenyans placed in line behind him. Warner discovered that all of these runners came from the same tribe of Kenyans known as the Kalenjin. One of several explanations offered was the realization that Kalenjin go through an initiation ceremony on their way to adulthood, a rite of passage that is all about enduring pain. Although there were differing versions of the rite, most entailed the elements of crawling nearly naked through a tunnel of African nettles, being beaten on the bony parts of the ankle, having knuckles squeezed together, and/or having formic acid from the stinging nettles wiped onto their most private parts to induce stinging. All of this led to the culmination of the ritual—circumcision with a sharp stick. During this process, the young males were obliged to remain absolutely stoic, unflinching. If any sounds of whimpering were made, the tribe would label them a coward and they would be stigmatized by the whole community. After circumcision, the boys went to a small hut to begin to heal, but when the time came they were summoned to leave the hut, running with all their might despite the pain being suffered. Warner surmised that this rite of passage ceremony whereby the journey to adulthood required the capacity to endure pain explained in part why so many Kalenjin became remarkable at long distance running where the task becomes "pushing through pain" in order to win the prize. In fact, the broadcast opined that Kalenjin runners may have a distinct advantage over other athletes because they grew up in a society that taught them to embrace pain as part of what it means to became an adult, as opposed to the Western journey toward adulthood that quite contrarily tends toward being pain-aversive.[5]

4. For a good listing and links to these rites of passage see the Wikipedia article, "Rite of Passage."

5. See Warner, "How One Kenyan Tribe."

Each of these rite of passage examples entails: (a) some form of separating from one's embeddedness in a childhood relational system; (b) a liminal phase usually involving instruction by elders in the community on some aspect of adult life and responsibilities; followed by (c) reincorporation back into the community with a different status, value to the community, and a different role to play in serving one's people.[6] We elaborate on these in the following, offering possible variations for use in crafting one's own rite of passage.

The Separation Phase

For most groups wanting to create a rite of passage, the separation phase will simply involve creating some way for a teenager to be taken out of their typical relational system for a period of time. In creating a trail camp experience, this involved taking teens to a National Park for a five-day backpacking trip. Being in the wilderness and exposed to nature heightens many aspects of a rite of passage—closeness to the earth, respect for Creation, heightened sensory experience, elimination of technology, exposure to the elements, etc. which all aid in creating a "thin space" that opens many teens to God in new and refreshing ways. Separation rituals can be as simple as saying goodbye to caregivers for the week or they can be made more elaborate with times of silence for reflection, guided meditation or prayer, or fostered through an examination created by older members of the group.

Gordon Dalby records the ritual of the Ibo in which the elders of a tribe on a particular night, along with the fathers of the boys in the tribe, gather fifty feet from a mother's door.[7] A drummer sets a beat and a man, the nmoo, wears a large mask representing the spirit that starts the initiation. The nmoo dances in the yard of the mother claiming the territory between her and the men who stand on the other side. At some moment the nmoo rushes ahead and pounds on the door calling forth the boy inside. It's the mother however who opens the doors and cries out into the darkness "what do you want?" The father then joins the entreaty of the elders yelling for the boy to come out. The act of separation then requires the boy to be willing to step out from behind his mother and face the spirit. When he does step forth, a chorus of masculine voices overwhelms the mothers cry signaling

---

6. Zahniser and Whiteman, *Symbol and Ceremony.*

7. Dalbey, "Recovering Rites of Male Passage."

that the mother's little boy has died. As the teen joins the other boys being initiated, he is said to be "born anew" as a son of the fathers.

I (Chris) have not witnessed Christian groups exemplify such powerful or dramatic imagination, but I have seen rites of separation done effectively. Different groups will need to decide how much to disclose about the ritual and its meaning while keeping certain aspects undisclosed so as not to undermine the elements of surprise. Readings and prayer can be encouraged prior to the separation. Questions can be asked individually or to the group to create a sense of anticipation and openness—"Are you willing to be changed? Are you willing to open yourself to whatever God may want to do through this experience? Are you willing to have others tell you the truth about what they see in you and seek to grow through whatever challenges they may present for you?" The process of gathering items for the experience can figure into part of the participation, and offering some article of clothing[8] (t-shirt, bandana) or a walking stick can be done with symbolic meaning of beginning a new journey. Some sacred rituals prepare the participants by including washing to signify purification. Other native Indian cultures utilize the sweat lodge—though this has been hazardous to some participants and should not be incorporated without experienced knowledge and the availability of medical assistance.

For trail camping, we typically divided the teens and our staff into groups of eight. Staff was made up of currently enrolled seminary students.[9] The ratio of three adults for every five youth provides a great balance of counselor to youth. In case of an injury or emergency, having three adults on hand is quite a relief, and it provides a generative formula of spiritual maturity in the group. We do however coach the leaders to not be zealous about evangelizing the youth, desiring instead to first build trust and community in which life stories can be confided. If the group sleeps outside, they can be positioned in a row with one adult flanking each side and another in the middle. This avoids shenanigans in the middle of the

8. See, for example, the sixteenth to eighteenth-century practice of "Breeching (Boys)," on Wikipedia.

9. Earning class credit provided incentive for seminary students in our experience. As a graduate-level class, they would meet for an intensive week before the teens arrived. We trained them, according to Dr. Joy's precedent, in developing a curriculum, writing the devotional and trail guides, first aid, and had them develop menus and purchase food for the trip. The one downside was that when the teens discovered the staff were being given class credit, it seemed to give some perception that there were other motivations beyond just pouring life into them.

night, especially if boys and girls are on the trip together. I have had youth groups or individuals ask if they can be in the same group or stay each night with their closest friend. There may be a rare occasion where this is necessary, but when a friendship network is completely imported into the initiation rite it tends to undermine the desired impact of moving from one group to another through a rite of passage. Allowing freedom to sit with friends at meal times and around the campfire each night typically provides enough contact and reassurances that assigning them to backpack with a designated group is usually well received.

Among the African peoples, the rite of separation was done to coincide with circumcision. Due to medical concern for traditional methods of circumcision, this practice is slowly dwindling, leaving most parents to choose a medical procedure in the confines of the hospital. While antiseptically preferable, circumcision looses its connection to a rite a passage as signaling adulthood. African families are now seeking to reclaim the rite without necessitating the physical act of circumcision, utilizing the years surrounding a young boy's sixteenth birthday as a time of seclusion and instruction through mentorship. Borrowing the Western "trail camping" model of adults mentors paired with young boys and girls, compressed ritual time can still be claimed away from the relational system of parents. Very similar rites of passage may be recreated by other immigrant populations, using familiar rites that are already in place within their communities. The important aspect of such rites is that they signify a separation phase both physically and psychologically.

Liminal Phase

The liminal phase of a rite of passage typically creates the space for conveying the meaning of the rite and for seeking transformative moments in the lives of teens. Instruction passes through relationships of high trust and/or high respect. In ancient rites of passage and still in many countries today, elders are appointed to be the transmitters of instruction or the chief storytellers. The nature of the instruction is moral and spiritual, calling forth responsibility, character and a vision for the role the young might play in their community in the future.

The delivery of the instruction can come about through a variety of means. Families have often turned birthday celebrations into rites of passage and invited teachers, friends, religious leaders, and other prominent members of the community to write letters or speak words of blessing over their teen. One campus minister I know, Daniel Curran (with Young Life at Berkely), made a practice of spending half a day with key students who were graduating from his ministry. During this time he would name all the gifts and graces that he saw in the particular student that he witnessed coming to fruition while also providing them with areas that he believed they would need to address and grow into if they were to optimize their effectiveness in adult life.[10] This very personalized form of mentoring/discipling mirrors the life of Jesus walking and talking with his disciples as they encounter missional settings together.

Indeed, given the level of dissonance experienced by children of first generation immigrants, a one-time/period of instruction is not sufficient. For these teenagers, the liminal phase may be designed for a longer process beyond the separation period for two to four years, once or twice a year as is feasible. It could be designed as a week away during summer or winter break and integrated with some fun events like sports, travel or retreat. Such a design offers the space for the teenagers to create meaningful bonds with one another and with their mentors. Relationship are key to effective mentoring and create the context for effective accountability. The actual content of the time away need not be exactly the same for each ethnic group. What matters is that relationships form to allow safe space, instruction, and deepening curiosity. Challenging open-ended questions are key to get teens thinking beyond their present circumstances.

On several trailcamp trips we utilized foot washing as part of a concluding evening ritual. We would set the group apart around a campfire, sometimes posing a question for them to answer:"What are the next steps you want to take in your walk with Jesus?"; "How has God become more real to you through this experience and how would you like to offer more of yourself to Him?" A good foundational premise to guide these considerations is that we look for multiple ways in programming across the teen and young adults years for repeated opportunities to "give as much of yourself as you understand to as much of God as you understand."[11] It is important however to monitor both an individual's and a group's threshold of commitment, so that the commitment you are seeking to solidify is

---

10. Daniel referenced this practice in a campus ministry seminar taught at Asbury Seminary in January 2004. He credited it to Jim Sylvester calling it a "street vision plan."

11. This was a foundational principle I learned during my campus ministry years under the leadership of Steve Moore at the Texas Tech Wesley Foundation.

not too heavy so as to become burdensome, rejected or unattainable; nor too light as to seem trivial or unworthy of commitment. We would then call out the name of a student and accompany them to a separate campfire. For those ready for the challenge, we would ask them a question like those posed above. After answering, a foot washing might follow in which the counselors who had led the group for that particular teen would speak words of truth and blessing, calling forth the good and painting an image of a positive future specific to what they had witnessed through the week together. Some secular and religious groups ask teens to fashion a Credo or faith statement giving articulation to the life and beliefs they intend to own as their own.[12] All of this can become the basis for establishing a covenant of commitment to guide teens beyond the rite of passage creating the basis for further accountability.

In ancient customs, storytelling often occurred around an open fire, richly symbolic with meanings of warmth, burning, ashes, ascending smoke, and light in the darkness that can be gleaned for deeper meanings. Our approach was to glean stories from the Scriptures, from personal testimonies, or from literature that would either tap into childhood wounds or places of suffering that the youth might be carrying or that helped teens imagine a life of future faithfulness and contribution. Dr. Joy built one camp experience around Rembrandt's painting of the Prodigal Son as experienced by Henri Nouwen's in his book, *Return of the Prodigal Son*.[13] Students would dress as still-life representations of one of the characters in the painting. After the story was read or retold, one-by-one the characters would step out of the picture and convey how they felt toward the prodigal as a brother, father, servant in the house, betrothed, etc. Inevitably, the stories for those in character became self-referential, and made for easy identification from the youth. As each character stepped out of the picture to convey their story, they were handed a story stick. After their story was dramatized the stick would be passed around the group. When the stick came into a teen's possession, they were given the opportunity to share feelings, memories of their own family related to the characters or other ways of responding to the story. If their reaction was too personal to share or in

12. For a secular version of this practice, see the Wikipedia article on "Jugendweihe," in reference to this movement in Germany. I learned a religious version of this from Dixie Robertson who would have our youth groups at First United Methodist Church in Lubbock, Texas, compose a Credo that was then framed and posted on the church walls celebrating each annual confirmation class.

13. Nouwen, *Return of the Prodigal Son*.

the rare occasion where the story did not connect, they could simply pass the stick on to the next person. As trust builds through the week, and as stories are structured toward evoking deeper levels of vulnerability, powerful contexts can be created.

In many rites, the ones being initiated are gathered together for the liminal period in settings apart from their community or family—a hut, sacred space outside the village, into the woods or dessert, border waters, a synagogue or church building. In Naga culture, a Morung house gathered boys and men in evening hours where wisdom was passed between generations. Most of the men would then retire to their homes while the budding young men slept in the house together.[14] I have read of a men's group that sends teen boys on a long hike through the woods. Every quarter mile a male parent from the youth group intercepts the youth and walks with them for another quarter mile, talking with them about a particular virtue essential for their adult life such as integrity, courage, fidelity, or perseverance.[15] The teen is then instructed to walk the next quarter mile alone while pondering the meaning and implications of what they just heard.

One important feature of many rites of passage is the inclusion of some sort of challenge during the liminal period in which the teen is "tested" and through which the teen demonstrates to themselves and to others a readiness for entering the next stage of life. In educational settings this is quite naturally structured as passing the necessary classes in the college or vocational curriculum. In religious settings, (sometimes referred to as "confirmation") the challenge is often to learn, recite or give evidence that knowledge of the primary teachings of one's faith tradition have been learned and owned. In some African cultures, the test given to boys historically involved displays of great strength or courage including the killing of a lion, enduring circumcision without flinching, or obtaining a kill from being on a hunt. In Ethiopia, the Hamar have maintained the custom of bull jumping in which young boys run back and forth across the backs of bulls or castrated cows, suffering ridicule if they fall. One

14. I owe this insight to Dr. Kwang Aier, provost at Shalom Bible Seminary in Kohima, Nagaland, who pointed it out after one of my presentations at the seminary in April 2018. Alivoker Aier subsequently published an article on the Naga Morung in the seminary journal (see Aier, "Re-visiting the Rich Cultural Practices").

15. Michael Gurian has travelled internationally and offered foci on various elements of rites of passage, including globally recognized virtues to elevate in such rites of passage. See more in his 1999 acclaimed book, *A Fine Young Man: What Parents, Mentors, and Educators Can Do to Shape Adolescent Boys into Exceptional Men.*

South American country asked young girls being initiated to run/walk as far as they possibly could into a predetermined direction providing a metaphor for endurance. The time returning from the trek is used for reflection to illicit the meaning of the run. South Pacific Islanders practice land diving. Reeds are tied to the ankles and wooden platforms are built from which young men jump head first akin to a primitive from of bungee jumping. Still others encourage fasting for several days, turning attention from physical gratification to spiritual discipline.[16]

In our backpacking adventures gleaned from Don Joy, part of the challenge entailed carrying a forty to sixty pound backpack for a five to nine mile hike through the forest each day. Other features were also built into the experience like sleeping under a tarp exposed to the elements or jumping off a twenty to thirty foot rock ledge into the river, or being without running water or flush toilets for several days. In Western litigious society it is imperative that medical information be collected before the trip, liability waivers signed, and some element of "challenge by choice" be built into these experiences.

I (Anne) recount what was known as the "presidential award scheme" that I was involved around age eighteen back in Kenya. The challenge created in this month-long project involved twenty-five hours of volunteer community work, two day of competitive sports, a camping hike over Mua hills for three days and a final essay that integrated our reflections from the experiences. We were divided into groups of five and each of us took on a responsibility as part of our small group. There was a group leader, two navigators, meal planner, and first aid person. Though our leadership roles were clearly demarcated, the actual work to accomplish any of the tasks was group executed. The challenge was that we were not given directions to where we were going, except for coordinate points on a map. It was the work of the group, guided by the navigators, to map the coordinates into a hiking route. At every coordinate point (about every ten miles), a staff person was stationed to clock in our time. Any group that missed their check point would have to track back and re-route. At the end of our day's trek, we would also be required to eat a cooked meal, prepared over a campfire, using ingredients and utensils that we carried in our back packs. This required the meal planner to manage three days of food for five people, distributing it to be carried in backpacks as manageable as possible. Normally, the final day's destination would be a school or church compound. Sleeping

16. See references to these ceremonies on the Wikipedia page, "Rite of Passage."

arrangements were well insulated sleeping bags on bare earth under the expansive night sky. Showers were an unreachable luxury. Required cooperation turned initial regret and unfamiliarity with the group to closeness and necessary team building. Completing the challenge scheme was rewarded with a silver award certificate. The deeper benefit was the growth to maturity that happened in one month—persevering through disappointment and physical hardships, mutual dependence on each other for our welfare, organizing and planning ahead all bonded me with friends I still hold dear thirty-one years later! What at the time seemed a strenuous physical challenge, turned out to be an exhilarating satisfaction that became the basis of my self-esteem and drive for achievement and spiritual reflection. The connection to the elements and humans that I depended on was such a powerful manifestation of meaningfulness of life.

Muslims are mandated sometime during their life to perform a Hajj, a pilgrimage, to Mecca if they are physically and financially capable and can support their family while absent. A series of rituals structure the journey, including: walking counter-clockwise seven times around the Kaaba—a building at the center of Islam's most holy mosque; running back and forth between hills that commemorate Hagar receiving water from Gabriel to rescue her son Ishmael; drinking from a sacred well; standing in vigil where Mohammed allegedly gave one of his last sermons; symbolically stoning the devil; shaving the head; making animal sacrifice; and celebrating a global festival.[17] There is a parallel tradition of pilgrimage in Christian tradition that may be incorporated into a rite of passage.[18] A further example is a pilgrimage included in a curriculum designed by Leader Resources titled Journey to Adulthood.[19] This well-designed program was initially established to refashion confirmation in the Episcopal Church but has been adapted for a number of different denominations. The curriculum begins with Rite 13, an acknowledgement of the arrival of pubescence and the gift of power to create that uses Psalm 113—"you are fearfully and wonderfully made"—to claim sexuality as part of God's intent and image in the teen. As a teen progresses through adolescents a team of mentors are set in place to avoid the teen experiencing adolescents

---

17. This information is drawn from the Wikipedia page, "Hajj."

18. See, for example, Thobaben, "Pilgrimage in the Christian Life," a chapel address by Dr. James Thobaben recorded at Asbury Seminary, November 16, 2016.

19. For more information about this resource, see LeaderResources, "J2A Training."

as a "tribe apart."[20] Focused teaching during these years target sexuality, spirituality, identity, community, and service. A unique feature of the curriculum is asking students toward the end of high school to customize a pilgrimage that intends two aims—to encounter God in a special way and to make an initial discernment of the spiritual gifts one has been given and how those gifts might be employed in serving the church. Once the pilgrimage is completed, teens are asked to give witness to why they fashioned their pilgrimage the way they did, how they encountered God, and how they hope to serve God and the faith community in their adult life. This portion of the curriculum is called *Young Adults in the Church*[21] and gives the community a viable way to bridge the transition into adulthood, support the leadership of young people in the church, and avoid the exodus of so many teens leaving church during this transition.

Quite often, when the challenge has been overcome or the time of instruction completed, symbolic gifts are given to the teen. These gifts are meant to bestow a new sense of identity on the recipient, signifying passage into the new group they are now entering, or extending a vision of becoming for the future. In one early version of the trail camp adventure, Dr. Joy would issue pocketknives to the teens creating spaces throughout the hike for them to carve symbols into the stick that represented salient and sometimes painful childhood memories. One night toward the end of the rite, these childhood walking sticks were surrendered into the fire while the passage from 1 Corinthians 13 was read, "when I was a child, I talked like a child, I thought like a child, I reasoned like a child. When I became a man, I put childish ways behind me." A new walking stick was then issued to signify the embrace of a new journey through adulthood.[22] Following are some of the gifts we have seen incorporated into rites of passage and what we believe they were meant to convey:

- Ilya Okhotnikov created a rite of passage for his daughter's sixteenth birthday. Prior to this time she was forbidden to cut her hair, adorn herself with jewelry, or wear high heel shoes. As part of the ceremony her mother presented her with a pair of pearl earrings as her father spoke about the way a slave in Biblical times would have their ear pierced to the portal of a Master's house pledging covenant fidelity to

20. LeaderResources, "J2A Training."
21. LeaderResources, "J2A Training."
22. Joy, *Empower Your Kids to Be Adults.*

the Master. Her mother also clasped a string of pearls around her neck symbolizing purity of heart, and her father placed high heels on her feet and allowed her hair to be cut. American culture tends to create in the minds of many teens that entrance into adulthood constrains freedom, the gifts that Okhotinikov's created inverted this meaning.

- Purity rings or similar symbolic gifts have been used in Evangelical circles to secure pledges of sexual purity until marriage. In cultures where high percentage of teens engage in non-marital sexual behavior such a pledge among peers may help create a Christian subculture of resistance. However, it is imperative that the community also convey that technical virginity is not the only reward and that we are all on a pathway toward sexual wholeness and healing.

- A house key symbolizes in some families the time when a child reaches the age and maturity to be left at the house alone. Car keys, drivers license, checkbook or credit cards often represent passage to greater independence. For many, a portion of what a rite of passage intends to communicate is the adage that "with greater freedom comes greater responsibility." The length of the leash depends on how trustworthy the recipient proves themselves to be.

- One of the traditions we have initiated in our family (Gatobu's) is a rite of passage ceremony as our boys turned eighteen, complementary to birthday and graduation. We invite our friends and family to write notes of advice, wisdom and encouragement. These are compiled into a three-ring binder (book) and presented as a communal gift to our eighteen year old. The ceremony also involves inviting select adults and friends of the teen to give a public speech of encouragement and wisdom to the child. On occasion we have incorporated a hand-washing ceremony where the father of the child symbolically gives over the child to a designated adult, familiar to the child but unrelated. The adult washes the child's hands, then dries them over a *rungu*, or "power stick," conveying a sign of power and responsibility bestowed on the teen as he or she embraces a new being of the self.

- A Journey to Adulthood (J2A)[23] spokesman described one congregation that had a number of quilters. This church decided to take fabric squares and fabric markers and ask the congregation to name memories, share important verses, or write blessings on the squares. The

23. See footnote 16 above.

squares were then fashioned into a quilt that was draped over each student in a service of worship celebrating their high school graduation. What many found was that the blankets were carried to their college dorm room. The inevitability of the quilt becoming a conversation piece provided an easy and early way for the college student to give witness to their faith and retain connection to their faith community.

Rites of Reincorporation

The final phase of a rite of passage occurs as the initiated person transitions back into their tribe or relational context. Don Joy believes that the critical components of an authentically transforming experience are contingent upon a young person being given a new status, a new value, and new role to play in the community.[24] Tribal rites of passage demarcated the movement from childhood to adulthood in ways that made these elevations clear—a boy was taken from the sphere of his mother's care, called out by the elders and sent through the challenges of the liminal period, and then repositioned among the men with a new set of expectations. To cite several examples; in the Vision Quest, a Native Indian boy might acquire a new name/identity based on the animal/totem that appears; an African boy once initiated is permitted/expected to go on the hunt acquiring a new role in his community. Kima Pachua, my colleague from the Miso tribe in Northeast India recounted that he felt his rite of passage into adulthood occurred when he was invited to participate with the men of the community in digging the graves for one who had died.

Research and observation have led many to believe that the rite of incorporation is often the missing piece in Western attempts of rite of passage, diminishing the impact of the experience. In our backpacking adventures we purposed for the teens involved to practice numerous acts of adult responsibility and care. These included care for creation—"pack it in, pack it out"; cooking and cleaning for each other—the first group back prepared the meal for the whole; building and tending a fire; setting up tents and camp for the evening; organizing clothes and food for your own pack each day; learning how to take intentional time for devotion and meditation, as well as sharing themselves among peers. We witnessed dramatic transformations through the week as youth felt respected and found roles to play that allowed them to contribute with each other. A key component

24. Joy, *Empower Your Kids to Be Adults.*

of the liminal period is the sense of *communitas*[25] that forms among peers as they encounter fears, faces challenges and celebrate victories together. Many of these could be effectually erased however when we returned teens to their families and they were placed back into the same relational system from which they came. Therapist will often talk about homeostasis—the tendency of family systems to resume established ways of behaving—even when this pattern has been dysfunctional for some members of the family. We think it is therefore important, where possible, that the family and/or other group into which the initiate is being promoted be brought on as a partner in honoring the new status, value and role being bestowed upon the teen through the rite of passage.

Mention of the ITAV Camps model once again comes to the fore. How much more powerful and effective would the liminal phase be if parents were simultaneously in their own retreats to discuss the changes they would need to make so as to embrace the re-incorporation process of the teen transitioning back into the system! A curriculum that runs parallel with an ITAV camp to prepare the parents for re-entry of their child would be excellent context nurture! This need not be as long as the children's ITAV camp but may actually be just a one day deal. The model is not new: In the book the *Anatomy of Peace: Resolving the Heart of Conflict*,[26] the Arbinger institute utilizes a very similar model where parents do not just drop off their kids at a camp in Arizona, but rather, they too are involved upfront in a three-day parents retreat. Here, parents wrestle with the roles they each have been playing to maintain and draw out the very negative behaviors they seek to extinguish in their children. They leave the camp with a greater understanding not only of their children's behaviors but also of their own self-reflective tendencies that work to maintain those behaviors.

In the Lutheran Church of my (Chris's) childhood, I entered confirmation around the age of twelve. What followed was a two-year period of instruction given by the pastor in which confirmands memorized and processes the Creed's, the Commandments, the Lord's prayer and other teachings of the church. My parents placed particular importance on confirmation, signified in part by the celebration and gift-giving at the culmination that rivalled any birthday party I had growing up. It was communicated to me that I now had voting privileges at church meetings and could attend any of the adult Sunday School classes that I chose.

25. For a good discussion of *communitas*, see Hirsch, *Forgotten Ways*.

26. Arbinger Institute, *Anatomy of Peace*.

It was not long thereafter that I was teaching Sunday school classes to younger aged groups—likely a pre-cursor to my role as professor today. There is formative power when a community understands their capacity to sponsor teens into adulthood through identity-bestowing ritual when these are not imposed on teens but are commensurate with their own readiness and visions of adulthood.

9

Immigrant Family Palavers or Indabas in Diaspora

—Tapiwa N. Mucherera

THE JOURNEY OF LIFE is never meant to be travelled alone. An African say-ing, "If you want to travel fast walk alone, but if you want to go far, walk together in the company of others or with someone," is true for how most Africans perceive the journey of life. When you walk alone, it is true that you will walk faster or at your own pace, but if you encounter problems you are alone to face the problems. Whilst when you travel with someone or others, if you face dangerous situations you know you have a helping hand. This truth is more evident when an immigrant moves to an individualistic cul-ture (in the Western world), especially coming from a communally oriented society. Many times one feels s/he is walking life alone when living in an individualistic Western context, particularly in times of need.

For many immigrants, moving makes them encounter loneliness and even depression. Who wants to live in a place where every time you meet someone new and after saying something, the first question the person asks you is: "Where are you from, I hear you have an accent?" In other words, the person has just told you, you are a foreigner to this land and you might even be an "illegal immigrant /foreigner." Depending on how the question is posed, the attitude is such that having an accent can be as bad as having a contagious disease. This does not matter how long one has lived in the Western world (this author has lived in the USA for over three decades and is still asked this question almost every week).

There are others however who ask the question about "accents" out of interest to create new relationships; and still others who ask because they feel one does not belong. Amazing that the USA is called "a nation of immigrants," yet these attitudes are still assumed towards immigrants. Lately, there has been the intention of new stricter laws being put in place by the President so as to have fewer immigrants enter the USA. Isn't it true that the only people who can claim rights to this land (N. America) are the Native American or Nation peoples and everyone else is an immigrant from somewhere? Yet, there are those whose parents immigrated here decades ago (and have lost their accents), who feel as though recent immigrants should not be allowed to stay and that they should go back to their native lands. How soon we forget that in the North America context, everyone came from somewhere except for the Native Americans? It is also amazing, however, that this is not a new phenomenon.

In Exodus God reminds the children of Israel that one of their social responsibilities was to be hospitable to strangers/foreigners, once they settled in the Promised Land. "You must not mistreat or oppress foreigners in any way. Remember, you yourselves were once foreigners in the land of Egypt" (Exod 22:21).[1] I believe the continued struggle we see between the Israelites and the Palestinians is the fact that one of these nations has forgotten that they were once foreigners at some point in their history.

Immigrants experience different phases of adjustment when they settle in a foreign land, even in cases where it is by choice that they moved to the new land. Initially, most experience a "honeymoon phase." This is the phase where one has renewed hope of accomplishing that which they had dreamed of, which they could not in their old environment. Both those who freely chose to immigrate and those who might have been forced to do so due to harsh conditions or found their lives in harm's way in their countries of origin, experience this honeymoon phase. If they were escaping an oppressive government or war, they feel as they have newfound freedom. Their anxiety about what tomorrow may bring is lower and they feel a little bit more in control than when they were in their countries of origin. If individuals immigrate as refuges, especially in the Western world, the communities that adopt them usually provide the immigrant refugees with the basic necessities. Eventually, this will come to an end as the refugee is now expected to get back on his/her feet and be self-sufficient.

Some of the immigrants will experience ambivalence. They love their new environment and yet miss much about their land of origin. These individuals may love the work they do, but may miss the relationships they

---

1. New Living Translation.

had in their former country. They are caught in between what they are able to accomplish, even feeling more productive, while also experiencing a void in their human relationships. Their relationships are very artificial since they are based on what they can produce rather than one who they are as a person.

And yet others after the honeymoon period may experience depression. Simple things such as not being able to find the types of foods that that they were used to can easily throw one into depression. Another cause of depression might be yearning for the old country, or lack of familiarity in the new land. For others it might be things did not turn out as they expected. In other cases, it is because of the treatment one experiences from other human beings; despite how much one may look similar and/or different. As humans, are we not supposed to celebrate diversity, one wonders, and isn't the fact that we are all humans a connecting factor for us? We live in a world today that is suspicious of "difference." Instead of people seeing difference as an opportunity to learn from the "other" that which is unfamiliar, it is looked upon as negative, abnormal, strange or deviant. Humans, though created by the same God, have become "indifferent" to one another, especially being "different ethnically."

When the period of excitement and "honeymoon" is over, reality sets in, which may cause a person to start questioning the decision of why they migrated. Those who are ambivalent start wishing they had listened to those from their home countries who might have tried to discourage them from migrating. They start questioning their decision-making abilities and shame may cloud their being. "You can never go back home," they think to themselves. Another percentage actually end experiencing deep depression, especially if one is living by themselves and the only meaningful contact is co-workers or schoolmates. If these co-workers or schoolmates are mostly North Americans it means the person has a very limited circle of friends or acquaintances. They will have to make appointments in order to be able to have meaningful relationships or fellowship with these co-workers or classmates. Otherwise, a person in such a situation can spend most of his/her time sheltered inside the four walls of his/her apartment or home. Most immigrants from communally oriented societies grow up with an open door policy or "open family systems," where people don't have to make appointments to visit each other. Moving from such an open system to a "closed system," one can easily be thrown into deep depression due to the lack of meaningful relationships. This holds true especially when someone is moving from a very close knit relational family network, to being plunged into a very individualistic closed system.

Life Is Lived in Community in Indigenous Contexts

That life must be lived in community is foundational to indigenous societies' philosophy of being and is true to many African contexts. In most African traditional societies, to deny one's community is to deny one's sense of self. One's "community of embeddedness" gives one a sense of who one is and help in time of need.[2] Mbiti, writing about the idea of community says; "Nature brings the child into the world, but society creates the child into the social being, a corporate person. For it is the community which must protect the child, feed it, bring it up, educate it and in many other ways incorporate it into the wider community. Children are buds of society, and every birth is the arrival of 'spring' when life shoots out and the community thrives."[3] The idea of the community giving a child an identity is widespread in many of the African societies. It is normal for people in a community to say, "this is our child" in reference to any child in the community, even though they may not be related by blood. Children are expected to give respect to the elders or adults in the community. They are taught not to call adults by their first names but as 'uncle' 'auntie' or "Mr." or "Mrs." so and so. The use of "auntie or uncle" does not connote any blood relations but is used as a sign of communal relations and of respect. However, the child is expected to listen to adults' instructions given that the community presumes such respect to be rendered. The common saying, "It takes a village to raise a child," is a shared practice still today especially in traditional settings. This may not hold true in the big cities and towns but would hold true especially in the rural areas where people are still more traditional in their values and practices. In the rural areas, people still put value in knowing who their neighbor is, even asking for "salt" from each other if they ran out.

Mbiti further says about the African understanding of person within community,

> In traditional life, the individual does not and cannot exist alone except corporately. He owes his existence to the other people, including those of past generations and his contemporaries. He is

2. Mucherera, *Counseling and Pastoral Care*, 68.
3. Mbiti, *African Religions and Philosophies*, 141.

simply part of the whole. . . . The community must therefore make, create, or produce the individuals, for the individual depends on the corporate group. Physical birth is not enough: the child must go through rites of the incorporation so that it becomes fully integrated into the entire society. These rites continue throughout the physical life of the person, during which the individual passes from one stage of corporate existence to another.[4]

The rites the community does in incorporating the child have an impact on the child's sense of self or identity. As stated in the above paragraph quoted from Mbiti, rituals are done at several stages of life. One of the first rituals practiced by most African communities is that of "bringing out the child" after birth:

The child has, however, begun its journey of being incorporated into the community, so that the separation between the individual mother and child continues to widen as the child's integration into the wider community also increases. . . . Paradoxically, then, the child is near the mother and yet begins to get away from the individual mother, growing into the status of being "I am because we are and since we are therefore I am." . . . The child is now public property, it belongs to the entire community and is no longer the property of one person. It has died to the stage of being alone in the mother's womb: but now it has risen in the new life of being part of the human society.[5]

These rituals serve as a reminder to the community at large that the child now belongs to them (community) to nurture and grow. The other rituals common in most indigenous contexts are initiation ceremony (from childhood to adulthood), marriage and finally death. These ceremonies and rituals become major markers of one moving from one stage or season of life to another. In addition, with each passing stage, a person is also moving from one hierarchy to another in the community. The older you become, the more a place of respect you are granted by the community. Note that, the moving from one stage to another means one is living in harmony with others as well as being a model citizen. The honor and movement from one stage to another comes with the duty of being a responsible community member. Oduyoye, an African woman theologian, suggests this when she notes:

4. Mbiti, *African Religions and Philosophies*, 141.
5. Mbiti, *African Religions and Philosophies*, 147–48.

> Africans recognize life as life-in-community. We can truly know ourselves if we remain true to our community, past and present. The concept of individual success or failure is secondary. The ethnic group, the village, the locality, are crucial in one's estimation of oneself. Our nature as beings-in-relation is a two-way relation: with God and with our fellow human beings.[6]

The sense of community according to Oduyoye, further encompasses not only human beings but also, all of creation including God. Harmony with God, nature and others therefore, becomes of importance to the individual's sense of self. This foundational understanding of self still prevails in most African communities especially in the rural areas.

The Impact of Colonization on Immigrants

Change started to impact indigenous context with the coming of colonization, urbanization and advent of Christianity. However, the change has not totally eroded the bedrock of this African understanding of community as much as one can readily see the impact of modernization and urbanization on the contemporary African society. Kapenzi, an African (Shona), writing on the clash of cultures in the African context, says,

> Conflicts between the old and the new social principles are producing new rivalries unknown in the traditional tribal order. Industrialization and urbanization have released new forces and created new groups. Members of a family are isolated more and more from each other. Men and women are taken far away out of their families and kinship groups, where they become involved with strangers within a whole system of impersonal institutions.[7]

The change that happened in these African societies still continues today (especially in the urban contemporary contexts). This has had an impact on the instability of the family by separating tight extended family systems by geographical distance. This is because most contemporary families (raised in urban areas) in Africa south of the Sahara today, tend to be more nuclear family focused. Some are living a life caught in-between the western and traditional cultures. They are neither fully African in their way of life, nor are they fully western. In other words, some can easily negotiate both (urban and traditional) cultures; others are torn as to which culture to follow.

6. Oduyoye, "Value of African Religious Beliefs," 100–101.

7. Kapenzi, *Clash of Cultures*, 47.

For those born in the African contexts, especially from the cities, who then immigrate to the West, they face greater challenges about who they really are in terms of identity. They are neither African-American by culture nor are they "truly African," since in their countries of origin they were not considered "African cultured." Imagine the so called "uncultured family" moving ten thousand miles away from their country of origin and immigrating to another country? The impact of this change proliferates the identity challenge of a child born to African immigrant parents or one (a child) who grew up in an African society who then migrates to a Western context. For those who are fully bi-cultural, it might be easier if they migrate. However, when crisis situations hit, they are forced to choose one over the other—the traditional way or western way to resolve problems. In most cases, individuals or families from the cities have better opportunities or access to migrating to the Western world. Some may be bi-cultural in their countries of origin or may be caught in-between cultures. It is even more challenging when these parents bring their own young children to raise in the Western world, or let alone if they start their families in the western world. Many of the parents themselves are caught in between cultures (bicultural) trying to raise the children to adapt to a new culture they themselves don't feel embedded or rooted in. The challenge is that they are bringing a "bi-cultural identity" to yet another third culture—meaning they are forced to create a *tri-cultural level of identity*.

A Tri-Cultural Identity: Complicated and Intricate

The Western world is extremely individualistic in nature and those who migrate, even those who used to live in urban settings in their countries of origin, have to adjust to a new way of living in the West. The immigrant parents are caught in a dilemma of how to raise their children; do they follow the Western values or do they go by the traditional communal or bicultural values they brought to the new context? The bigger question is; which culture are they to pass-on to their children, traditional or bi-cultural? In, addition, the questions is, which *bi-cultural orientation*—the one from the country of origin or of the Western world? Better still is the question of which culture their children belong? Sue and Sue writing about minorities in North America, (especially the Native Americans) posit that there are five different types of cultural orientations that native people experience.

1. Traditional: The individual may speak little English and practice traditional customs and methods of worship.

2. Marginal: The individual may be bilingual but has lost touch with his or her cultural heritage yet is not fully accepted in the mainstream society.

3. Bicultural: This person is conversant with both sets of values and can communicate in a variety of contexts.

4. Assimilated: The individual embraces only the cultural *mainstream* (Western) values.

5. Para-traditional: The individual has been exposed to and adopted *Western* values but is making a conscious effort to return to the old ways (traditional values).[8]

The immigrant parents are usually bicultural when leaving their countries of origin, meaning, their biculturalism is based on the level of westernization that occurred while in their countries of origin before they migrated. When they immigrate to the Western world, their biculturalism faces other issues such as racism, etc. As much as they migrate to the West as bi-cultural, they actually find that the new cultural environment throws them in the category of being marginalized. Racism and other factors, dictates a new paradigm shift in their self-identity, in that they neither fit the new western culture nor the Western context's bi-culturalism. The new context pushes some to choose assimilation as a way to survive, fit or adapt into the new environment. Sue and Sue say the following about the marginalized and the assimilated:

> They may face issues such as (a) lack of pride in or denial of "native" heritage; (b) pressure to adopt "Western" cultural values; (c) guilt over not knowing or participating in the "native or indigenous culture; (d) negative views regarding "natives or indigenous people"; and (e) a lack of an extended "family" support or belief system.[9]

The above stated by Sue and Sue is also true as experienced by those who migrate to the Western world. Many have to choose to assimilate or be marginalized in order to make "life" work. As stated earlier, this can result

---

8. Sue and Sue, *Counseling the Culturally Diverse*, 387.

9. Sue and Sue, *Counseling the Culturally Diverse*, 387.

in some experiencing depression, hopelessness, wishing to return to their countries of origin and/or even being suicidal.

This chapter tries to address the questions about how immigrant families or individuals can survive in a western world culturally, using palavers, given that the pressures to survive are stacked against them. For immigrant parents, there is not one homogeneous culture that holds everyone in their nuclear family together. The parents themselves may not have one "culture of embeddedness" and also find themselves caught in a "third culture."

Children born in the West to immigrants and/or those who immigrated as children find themselves caught in competing cultures, Western and bi-culturalism. They have to develop a "tri-level identity" in order to function. Their identity is no longer bicultural, since they find that they are caught in trying to negotiate between two "bi-cultural(s)"—that is the Western context bi-culturalism and the bi-culturalism they encounter in their immigrant parents. The level of identity of immigrant children would be truly multicultural; however, in this book the cultural orientation is indicated or named as "tri-culturalism or *tri-cultural identity*" since multiculturalism has other connotations of inter-cultural marriage. The immigrant children and parents being referred to are of the same ethnic heritage. The immigrant children have to learn to navigate three cultures instead of negotiating between two cultures, as their parents who might be bicultural would do. The children, therefore, unknowingly develop or live into *a tri-level culture* as a way to adapt.

For those who find themselves serving this population, there are other identity issues to pay attention, in that every individual is the same as other humans, yet very different. I agree with Kluckhohn, who says,

> Every man [sic] is, in certain respects, (a) like all other men, (b) like some other men, (c) like no other man. He [sic] is like all other men. . . . There are common features in the biological endowments of all men, in the physical environment they inhabit, and in the societies and cultures in which they develop . . . as a member of a society. . . . As social animals, men must adjust to a condition of interdependence with other members of their society and of groups within it, and, as cultural animals, they must adjust to traditionally defined expectations. . . . The human species would die out if social life were abandoned. Human adaptation to the external environment depends upon that mutual support which is social life; and, in addition, it depends upon culture. . . . Human beings, however, learn not only from experience but also from each other. All

> human societies rely greatly for their survival upon accumulated learning (culture). Culture is a great storehouse of ready-made solutions to problems which human animals are wont encounter. . . . Finally, there is the inescapable fact that a man is in many respects like no other man. Each individual's modes of perceiving, feeling, needing, and behaving have characteristic patterns, which are not precisely duplicated by those of any other individual.[10]

Anyone working with immigrant families or individuals has to take into consideration the factors mentioned above by Kluckhorn. The helper has to consider the basic human similarities, the cultural facts about each family or individual and yet have to be highly cognizant or mindful of the individual differences in each person, even a within nuclear family. This is where it gets complex and intricate when working with individuals or immigrant families, in that one is faced with the question of which cultural orientation to apply with each particular individual or family.

Immigrants Problem-Solving Technics in the Western World

When there are problems in the family in Western cultures, it calls for therapy or counseling. The way counseling or therapy is practiced in the West is very different from the way indigenous contexts practice counseling.[11] In the Western world, counseling or therapy is more individualistic as opposed to indigenous contexts where the resolving of a problem is more family or communal in approach. In indigenous contexts, if there is a problem for an individual, family or community, the general approach is that people come together and face the problem together rather than paying someone (a stranger for that matter) who is an expert to help resolve a family or personal problem. It has widely become recognized that some of the Western approaches to counseling do not serve those from the indigenous contexts well. Safransky, also a Western psychotherapist, offers the following critique about therapy as practiced in the West:

> Therapy has become a kind of individualistic, self-improvement philosophy, a romantic ideology that suggests each person can become fuller, better, wiser, richer, and more effective. . . . There are many who have located the roots of the therapeutic movement in the individualism embraced by the nineteenth-century

10. Murray and Kluckhohn, *Personality in Nature, Society, and Culture*, 53.
11. Mucherera, *Counseling and Pastoral Care*, 17.

> modernism, in which everyone is the author of his or her inten-
> tions and is responsible for his or her own life. Own. Own is a very
> big word in therapy; you own your life, as if there's a self, an indi-
> vidual, enclosed self, within a skin. That's individualism. That's the
> philosophy of therapy. I question that. The self could be redefined,
> given a social definition, a communal definition.[12]

The critique offered above by Safransky speaks in general to the way most immigrant parents who come to the Western world would perceive therapy or counseling. Thereby, it is common that if there are problems in a family, the family is lost on what to do. There is no traditional family or community to surround them in resolving their problems. Further, the individual Western approach of going to see a stranger to help resolve their problems is perceived with suspicion. How might a stranger, who does not know their cultural values and practices, help resolve the family problems? In the event that there are rituals to be performed, of which the stranger (counselor or therapist) may not be aware, what practical solutions will be offered? This renders the services of counseling in the western context for immigrant families as incomplete and incompatible. This then calls for a different method or paradigm to resolving family problems. Once in a while there are cities in the USA where one may find trained counselors from different parts of the world. For example, as there is much diversity in African cultures, these types of counselors may understand African immi-grants family or an individual's issues better. In circumstances where there are no trained indigenous counselors, it is better for African families to create family palaver for the purposes of problem solving.

Family Palavers

Counseling or therapy in indigenous contexts is more than "talk therapy." As mentioned earlier, it might involve rituals that include not just an in-dividual being counseled, but the participation of the family and or com-munity as a whole. The point being posited in this chapter is that *family palavers* might be the best alternative to serving individuals or families of immigrants, rather than seeking counseling from individual experts who are at times perceived as strangers to the culture as well as to the family. Given the cultural differences between the Western world and the commu-nally oriented societies, palavers will likely prove to be a better alternative.

12. Safransky, "Psychotherapy," 52–53.

As stated earlier, I agree with the idea earlier stated by Kluckhorn that as much as all human beings are the same, there are significant differences based on cultural and individual dissimilarities. Given what has been argued above, noting the differences between indigenous and the western culture, there is usually an impact on individual and family world-views. What then are these family palavers, and in what way can they be helpful to individual and immigrant families? Family palavers are still common among traditional and indigenous societies:

> A palaver (*padare or "indaba"*) is an informal or (formal) gathering usually for the purposes of providing counsel and support for those facing a personal, family, and/or community crisis and problems, and sometimes for the purposes of education and to share joys.[13]

Palavers (*indabas or dare*) can take different forms. They can be in form of nuclear, extended family, or community gatherings mostly with the goal of resolving a problem. In many cases they can be open or closed depending on the type of issues being discussed or needing resolve. Community or family elders preside over these types of gathering. The purpose of a palaver—*indaba/dare* is to find a common solution that those involved will agree upon or will take on as a resolution to the problem. One of the main advantages of a *palaver* is that everyone involved in the discussion circle has a voice. As long as one is included as part of the circle that is discussing the problem, one is expected to be part of the solution or working against the problem. The role of the elder(s) is to moderate and manage the discussion in making sure that all voices are heard and respected.

Family Palavers to Resolve Adult Issues

When we place the method of palaver in the USA context, one has to find two or three families, usually from the same continent with many similar values. The two or three families are encouraged to then come together to form an *indaba/dare or palaver* at a retreat center setting or hotel. This would best function at a neutral place, and not at someone's home. A neutral place helps put everyone on equal footing as opposed to being in someone's house where the host may feel some form or entitlement or "turf control." Depending on the type of issue being addressed, the families can

13. Mucherera, *Meet Me at the Palaver*, ix.

also invite an agreed-upon outsider—an elder from a similar culture but not from within the family, to be the moderator or presider. This helps to provide neutrality, bias or prejudgment, since the presider is someone only interested in helping resolve the problem(s) rather than taking sides. The different families all work against whatever problem is presented.

As is generally believed in narrative counseling or therapy, whatever issues there are to be resolved, "the person is not the problem but the problem is the problem." So, the idea is to tackle the problem, not the persons or personalities involved. This does not mean that a person is not held accountable of their actions, if their behaviors are contributing to the problem, but that the main goal is to resolve the problem. Sometimes the solutions call for individuals to change their behaviors or attitudes, and other times the people (system) around the person, has to change. At the palaver, it is recommended that those who are in conflict or have brought their problem to others don't sit together, but at opposite ends of the room for the sake of peace. People are given their turn to speak without interrupting the other(s). This is the job of the elder(s) who moderates.

Palaver sessions, similar to Western court systems can go on for hours or days, then be adjoined and people get back on the issue. Within the context of the North America, usually if this is dedicated to a weekend, the whole problem may not be resolved in that one weekend, but it is likely that most of the main issues will be solved and the people are given homework to continue working on the problem. If much is not accomplished, then the families can plan on coming back together to continue working on the issue(s). The main goal of the palaver is to resolve problems and not to attack individuals, personalities and/or character assassination.

The common issues immigrant adults face, especially couples or families, have to do with marriage, sharing of household chores or responsibilities, finances, raising of children in a different culture, unfaithfulness in the marriage relationship, intimacy, power and poor communication. Most of these couples usually tend to work very hard to make it in the new country with the goal of making a better life for themselves and especially for their children. However, many end up sacrificing time or relationships with their spouses or with their children. They can buy their children the latest gadgets or fashion, but lack a good relationship with their children. The same applies to the spouses; they don't intentionally create time for each other because they both are so tired from working double or triple strenuous shifts, and eventually growing apart in intimacy. When they get home all they want is to sleep, (probably for three hours) before they get on to another shift. They work hard for material things but lack solid, intimate, meaningful relationships with the spouse or children. These families become slaves to work as a way to make it up the ladder, at the expense of everything else of what it means to be human. They forget that as humans we are *primarily* created for relationships (with God and others) and *secondarily* to be stewards of the earth, which is where work comes. In the lives of the immigrant, work has become *primary*, and relationships have become secondary.

Family Palavers to Resolve Youth/Young Adult Issues

When dealing with issues pertaining to the youth or young adults, it is better to involve a youth or young adult together with another elder as moderators. This accomplishes three things: (1) the elder brings experience and knowledge to problem-solving, usually lacked by youth or young adult; (2) the youth or young adult gains experience by being mentored into the processes of the palaver; and (3) the youth/young adult will help present a different world-view, (especially a perspective of the younger generation) that older adults may miss. In all cultures there is always "a generation gap" and the youth or young adults being involved in the process help in "bridging that gap." It is common to hear older adults make such statements as "the youth these days are different and not easy to understand." Sometimes you also hear statements a "this younger generation is uncultured." This is usually in comparison to the older generation's culture and worldviews.

Culture is not static, it's dynamic, and so it is not surprising that each generation has it's own point of view different from the other. The gap is widened by the fact that in this twenty-first century, social media has changed how people relate. The younger generation can have over a thousand "friends" on Facebook, WhatsApp, Instagram, LinkedIn, Twitter, etc., who they may never meet in person for many years. These relationships are not personal; at best they are superficial, meaning the personal touch in interpersonal relations has now been changed significantly. When one is dead, unless someone pulls down the Facebook page, the person can continue to be counted as a friend (from their grave). True friendship no longer mean the same as understood by the older generation.

"Intimacy," with the introduction of pornography, has also been highly affected and no longer means the same as in the past. Who knew that an individual can become intimate with a picture or image on a screen, to the extent of being addicted to that "screen image/picture?" Marriages can end in divorce, and people go to prison or loose their jobs due to being addicted to screen images. The younger generation's mind is now wired differently from that of the older, especially on how intimacy is viewed. With the younger generation, one does not have to be necessarily present in the same place, in order to be intimate. The screen image or the person on the other side of the screen can be "intimate" without being physically present.

Education systems are no longer primarily face-to-face; rather one can learn from sitting in front of their computer screen and by "Googling." The generation today is born with access to computers and they know how to use them as young as two years old. Many have information but lack experience. It's a generation that believes that solutions are at one's figure tips, so if one has a problem, they just have to "google" it to resolve it. This shows how complicated problem solving for the younger generation can be, since relationships and understanding of life in general have changed. The challenge is that humans are not robots or mechanical beings; rather, they are *relational beings*, so one cannot resolve life relational problems by "googling" the solutions. It is a generation that is advanced in scientific ways of resolving problems, but is very poor or lacks the skills to resolve interpersonal relational problems.

This further complicates the situation when one now introduces the issues of a "third culture child" into the picture. The child is trying to negotiate several cultures: the parents' culture, the Western culture, their experiences in schools, that of the communities they live, and that which is presented to them through the media (both social and TV). This is why it is helpful for the youth or young adults to be part of the moderating team when holding a palaver meant to resolve youth or young adult issues. This generation of immigrant youth and young adults sometimes struggle with issue of identity, peer pressure; use of drugs and alcohol, religion, sexuality, which may lead into a struggle with a low sense of self-esteem. In order to try to fit into the culture, some try to please their peers so as to be accepted creating tension with their parents.

Palaver for Prevention and Family Maintenance

Many families or individuals have the tendency to wait to resolve problems after the problem has mushroomed or grown out of hand, to where there might be communication breakdown in the family system. The palaver can be used as a preventive measure; that is before problems skyrocket or gone out of control. Using the same approach, two or three families can come together for a weekend to simply check in and see if there might be issues that are emerging that may need attention before developing into bigger problems. This is done in a relaxed atmosphere and most people's anxieties are low because there are no specific problems being resolved other than prevention and maintenance. In other words, this is a call for families to "check in with each other before things fall apart." These sessions could be called CQI (continuous quality improvement) for the family relations. They could also be named QEP (Quality Enhancement Plan) sessions. These are session to check what might need attention in the family relations. One does not take their car to the mechanic only when it has developed problems. Neither should one wait to go to the doctor or dentist only when we have developed problems. The palaver is meant for maintenance of, and preventative care to family and individual relationships. When these families meet at the maintenance or preventative palaver, such questions as; what is going on well in our relationships and what is it that we may need to pay attention to, before developing into a big problem? In other words, are there some squeaky wheels that we may be ignoring that need greasing? Everyone including the children are given an opportunity to say their opinions.

These palavers are also opportunities for the adults to actually teach their children and younger adults some general life skills. The adults also model how relational issues are handled, self-respect and dignity, and issues of boundaries. These are opportunities where the kids can talk about what they are good at, what they want to do when they grow up, and name some of their dream colleges or schools. Many immigrant parents, when they first land on the western soil see education to qualify for office jobs, etc., only as a goal and priority for them and their children. They usually discourage their children from sports, but to focus on book knowledge. It is true that book knowledge is very important and must be emphasized for immigrant children; however, those parents who prevent their children from participating in sports may be at fault. These preventative palavers can help especially those parents who are totally oppose to sports and other extra-curricular activities for their children, to see that every child is gifted differently and that there are scholarship for sports, to support children to go to college as well. Palavers can be very helpful as an opportunity for parents to talk to their children before things or life starts happening.

This chapter has tried to give a synopsis of the development of the *tri-culture identity*. The problems immigrant parents and children face in the Western world can be helped by the use of the family palavers. These family gatherings cane be used as a way to counter problems before they take root. Palavers can also be a mentoring tool to be used by the future generations.

10

Concluding Observations

—Chris Kiesling

Quantitative analysis of migration movements gives a preliminary estimate that some 316 million people today are living in diaspora movements.[1] At just above 4 percent of the world's population, this indicates that one out of every twenty-five people in the world lives away from their country of origin. Ralph Winters comments that "most of the world's population can no longer be defined geographically."[2]

Our attempt in this volume has largely been to adopt a psychosocial approach to understand the unique identity conflicts that emerge for immigrants from various parts of the world as they attempt to acculturate to what has historically been the largest host country in the world, the United States of America. Our aim was not to be comprehensive, but rather to select authors who represented many of the major ethnic populations that have migrated to North America. By doing so, we felt we could offer a personalized account of the layered conflicts that immigrants to the United States encounter at the intersection of their own developmental journeys (first level identity crisis), the social-structural aspects that exists in American culture whereby every immigrant experiences being a minority (second level identity crisis), and the values embedded in their families reflecting their country of origin (third level identity crisis).

In this concluding chapter we want to offer observations, theoretical perspectives and categorical analysis that provide summation and offer possible directives for the future. Chapters in this volume have made it clearly

1. Tira and Yamamori, *Scattered and Gathered*.
2. Tira and Yamamori, *Scattered and Gathered*, 8.

evident that the experience of immigration and its attendant identity crisis, is far from homogenous—differing widely for people who share the same country of origin, ethnicity, or destination. Yet, generalizing across populations, looking for patterns and finding common elements of experience allows us to name social phenomenon. Naming helps us understand ourselves and others better, creating the possibility for increased empathy and development.

An Early and Popular Model of Acculturation

A four-fold model of acculturation has found popularity that many attribute to the work of John Berry.[3] This model is based on two dimensions: *cultural maintenance* and *contact participation*.[4] Cultural maintenance indicates the extent to which individuals consider it to be of value to maintain their cultural identity. Contact participation indicates the extent to which individuals consider it to be of value to have contact with those outside their own group, hence wishing to participate in the daily life of the larger, host society. Creating a yes or no continuum along these two dimensions produces a four quadrant diagram with the following description of each quadrant:

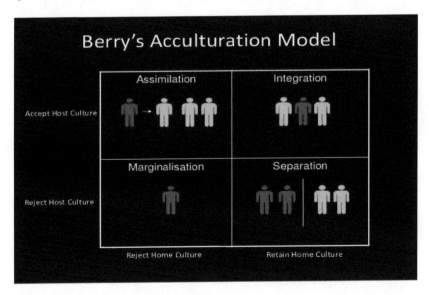

---

3. See, for instance, Berry, "Immigration, Acculturation, and Adaptation."
4. See the Wikipedia article, "Acculturation."

- *Assimilation*—acceptance of the host culture but rejection of the home culture results in a relinquishment of one's cultural heritage to maintain relationships with those in the host culture

- *Integration*—acceptance of both the host and home cultures produces a posturing to maintain characteristics of both cultures

- *Marginalization*—rejection of both the home and host culture results in the loss of both cultural and psychological resources for identity formation

- *Separation*—rejection of the host culture reinforces identification with one's home culture resulting in segregation

Whereas any model or theory offers at best a partial and oversimplified understanding of reality, Berry's categorization elevates the salience of navigating between cultures indicative of many of the narratives in this volume. Several of our authors described feeling "between two worlds," living in a state of "liminality" or wrestling with where they might find a sense of belonging. In many ways, our characterization of a second-level identity crisis precipitated by being a minority in the United States predicts that most immigrants have experiences of marginalization and segregation. American culture, historically emerging from bloody battles over slavery, imposes a racial consciousness on immigrants often foreign to the way they have always identified themselves. Salient was our African author who came to the shocking realization filling out forms for American customs that required her for the first time in her life to be identified by the color of her skin, not by the tribe or clan to which she belonged. Poignant was the commentary of our Asian author regarding the Korean student who went on a shooting rampage in Virginia, fearing that the societal ascription would further denigrate the perception of Asians in America. Layered on top of the normative developmental task of identity formation (first level), immigrants to the United States live in minority status subject to discrimination, stereotyping and prejudice (second level). As one of our authors expressed so well, living in a conflictive social context as a minority accentuates and reinforces differences that hardens ethnic boundaries and heightens group consciousness in ways that presage Berry's quadrants of marginalization or separation. This is especially true when the absence of legal status circumscribes the space and limits the opportunities for contact with the host culture. It appears from the contributions of our various authors that because White privilege is so embedded in American

Culture, the greater the contrast in skin color to white, the more difficult this is to overcome. The attempt to distance oneself via making ethnic distinctions—e.g., "Kenyan American verses African American" bespeaks of one identity strategy. One of our authors described the dilemma of how to hyphenate her self-description, recognizing that too much emphasis on either her host country or her country of origin could be misconstrued as betrayal or misrepresentation. Another author described immigrants in his ethnic population choosing different self-designations depending on their place of birth and/or the age at which they relocated. Similarly, other immigrants use descriptors that give emphasis to their ethnic origin hence downplaying racial differences. Nonetheless, most immigrants recount stories of encountering institutional policies and practices that unfairly favor those of European descent.

Motivational Factors

More recent theoretical attempts to distinguish among different groups of immigrants places emphasis on the motivational factors for migrating. Push factors infer a compelling reason to leave one's country of origin (absence of job opportunities, persecution, inadequate medical care, substandard housing, racial or ethnic discrimination, lack of political or religious freedom, genocide, violence, natural catastrophe). Pull factors infer an attraction to a country of destination (job opportunity, better living conditions, opportunities for education and health care, family ties).[5] These motivations, complicated further by whether one's migration is voluntary and involuntary, no doubt serve as determinants of how the task of identity formation is enjoined and navigated in a new location. In general, we might predict that a prevalence of pull factors would correlate with probable outcomes of assimilation and integration since the overarching motivation is to acquire the benefits of American culture; push factors may show a higher prevalence in outcomes of separation and marginalization as one is forced to leave a country often against their will and with hopes of eventually returning to the host country. This is an untested finding and represents a lot of generalizing, but we could at least speculate that push and pull factors are important influences on the acculturation process, serving as predictive precursors for how the identity crises is enjoined. Push and pull factors may also be determinative of how potently one experiences cultural shock

5. Tira and Yamamori, *Scattered and Gathered.*

so endemic to the immigrant experience, and how alienated one feels from meaningful community once settled in the host country.

Acculturation Stressors that Contribute to the Third Level Identity Crisis

The greatest contribution that we might offer from this volume however may be in chronicling the various components of what we have termed the "tri-level identity crisis" as a way of reifying the complexity of pyscho-social struggle for immigrants to the United States. Gleaning from our chapters, we offer the following, not as a comprehensive list, but as an initial naming of acculturation stressors symptomatic of what constitutes a tri-level identity crisis:

- *Attachment disruptions*—immigration for many entails the separation of parents from children and/or the separation from extended kin. This can come about in a variety of ways with varying degrees of both immediate and long-term consequences (e.g., immigration laws; one parent migrates first; termination of life via war, gang violence, natural disaster or human trafficking, etc.). Research, especially neurobiology, is debunking the myth that trauma at an early age is less devastating than later in life, establishing instead that adverse childhood experiences increase the likelihood of an array of social and health problems across the lifespan including the impairment of cognitive functioning.

- *Undermining of family as the epistemological base of identity*—Across the board immigrants name the family as the foundational structure for identity in their country of origin. Reinforced by cultural teachings of filial piety, respect for elders, honoring of ancestors, or the valuing of community, the general tendency seems to be that the more invested immigrants are in traditional views the more difficulties occur in acculturation in the West. Turmoil sometimes accrues to children who violate an implicit agreement with parents—we sacrificed for you as parents in expectation that you would respect and honor us in such things as the way you behave, educational accomplishments, who you marry, etc. Repeatedly in these narratives we hear about family cohesion being undermined when Western individualism compels young immigrants to disaffect from parental authority, finding affiliation and seeking information about self from other sources.

- *Identity assault via loss of occupational status*—particularly poignant in several of our testimonies are adults whose status within a culture radically changed after migrating. Occupational and educational attainments that augured positions of honor in their host country, counted for less or were not recognized in the United States, forcing them into less desirable and low-paying work roles. Identity is diminished when society reflects no openings for the gifting an adult seeks to bring.

- *Impoverishment and insecurity of resources*—acculturation stressors are often interrelated and influence one another. Parents who suffer a loss of status can be both psychologically and financially impoverished. Immigrants with strong educational backgrounds and opportunities in America typically assimilate well, but those with less educational background and diminished legal status often find their fears and deprivations compounding. Public school teachers become more adept at guiding children than do their parents, who for a variety of reasons may never avail themselves of support and resources.

- *Confounding of family roles*—For many, the process of immigration requires parents to relinquish or to acquire a different constellation of roles than would be typical in their country of origin. Women function as head of the household and breadwinners, men become absent fathers, kids are left alone or take care of young siblings while both parents work. Reflected in our collected stories of immigrants is the common experience of acculturation dissonance—children tend to assimilate more readily than their parents. Hence, for many young immigrants the reference point for who they hope to become may no longer be located in their parents, scrambling elsewhere to look for authority figures for with whom they can identify.

- *Seductions of American culture and default individuation*—When parents can no longer serve as referent points for who a child is trying to become, it is tempting and natural to look toward idealized images of popular American culture for imitation. Finding individuation through hair cuts, name brand clothing, fashion, or athletic shoes may gain popularity through the teenage years but outsourcing identity to name brands undermines the more important work of developmental individuation. Furthermore, parents suffer not only the loss of respect from children, but encounter further demoralizing if they feel inadequate and overly restrictive in relation to what their child regards as essential to social development.

- *Feeling deleted from the digital world*—currently nine in ten Americans are on-line indicative of a culture thoroughly immersed in technology. Many immigrant parents are not digital natives; and some are without resources, language acquisition, or know-how to navigate the world of technology. Their children's consumption of the internet then goes unmonitored and leaves them feeling left behind. With few restrictions on usage, the results can range from depression to gaming disorder to exposure to precocious sexual behavior.

Toward Pro-Social Identity Resolutions

Social anthropologist sometimes refer to the experience of immigration as living in liminal space. Re-appropriating this term from our chapter on rites of passage, liminality captures the sense of being "in-between." For many this creates the dilemma of "neither-nor." Disaffiliated from one's culture of origin, one *neither* feels fully at home in their host culture; *nor* does one feel that they fully belong to or can fully embrace the values of the country of destination. Some have suggested that real change begins to happen in one's internal acceptance when the "neither-nor" begins to be reframed and experienced instead as a *"both-and."* In this posturing, one holds the vestiges from the country of origin as an appreciative part of the self, constituting in some ways the DNA of who they are; at the same time recognizing that they are not a tree simply transplanted on foreign soil, but that the country of destination has also been grafted into what makes up the essence of who they are.

We begin this volume drawing from Erikson's theory of identity crisis to introduce the potentially perilous nature of what we termed "tri-level identity crisis." Erikson was particularly concerned about paradigms that posited people as fragmented individuals, separated from one another, and inactivated by the diffusion of their identity. Alternatively, he sought for conceptual ways to convey the possibility for unity and wholeness of personhood, acknowledging as we would, that spirituality often provided a profound and comprehensive way of structuring the self around a center of wholeness.[6] Erikson's image found articulation in such concepts as:

6. Hoare, *Erikson on Development in Adulthood.*

- actuality and mutuality—the release of defensiveness naturally acquired in attaining autonomy that frees one to participate and share effectively

- leeway—the freedom to be oneself and to grant such freedom to others

- adaptation—the move from passive acceptance of unacceptable life conditions to ego strength whereby one gains the power to fit the environment to one's needs and the needs of others

- insight—truth gained via contemplation of seeing into oneself and into a situation that obliges one toward ethical action

- virtue and centrality—the spiritual and ethical center that with optimum resolution of life stages allows the self to be bound together around transcendent values of hope, purpose, fidelity, love, wisdom, etc.

For Erikson, the resolution of any life stage allowed the possibility of acquiring a particular ego strength or virtue. For adolescents the desirable outcome was *fidelity*—a clarified sense of who and what could be entrusted with one's loyalty.[7] Of keen interest to Erikson were those historical persons whose resolution to their own profound identity knots became generalized to society in such a way that they became instruments of societal change. Might it be possible that some of those described in these pages could indeed be the culture-makers of the future. Living through the troublesome crucible of their own identity perplexities that they find the ego strength and virtue to help us navigate through the turbulent waters of immigration, diversity, globalization and shared economies into a more peaceable world in the future? As one of our authors named it, moving from "in-between," and "in-both" to "in-beyond."

Reading through the varied narratives reflected through the writing of the various authors that contributed to this book, I recalled a metaphor used by Linda Pearce and Melissa Denton some years ago in their book, *A faith of their own.*[8] Working to describe the faith journeys of American adolescents through the metrics of religious conduct, religious content and centrality, Pearce and Denton proposed that identity can be thought of as a mosaic of various colored tiles. Adapting this to our analysis, a particular tile might represent any of the various elements or domains that form a particular individual's sense of who they are (e.g., ethnicity,

7. Hoare, *Erikson on Development in Adulthood.*

8. Pearce and Denton, *Faith of Their Own.*

gender, religious belief, family relations, love, work, friendship, etc.). The shade of any particular tile would be indicative of the intensity of that identity element in the perception of an individual. Available tiles might be constituted by what a person's former or current social contexts offer to the them. The number of any particular colored tile could represent the extent to which a person regarded that element as an important dimension of how they see themselves.

The value of this metaphor is not only the nuanced richness that can be thought that each person possesses in their kaleidoscope of colored tiles, but also in the implicit sense that there is the possibility of agency and fluidity in how a person positions each tile and how each tile is assembled in relation to the larger image of what is being portrayed. As editors of this volume, we are grateful to the authors and the subjects who have allowed us to peer for a short time through their kaleidoscope, and we hope that the publication of this volume can contribute to better understanding, acceptance and appreciation of what has been seen.

Bibliography

Abedi-Anim, MeCherri Denise. "Bound by Blackness: African Migration, Black Identity, and Linked Fate in Post-Civil Rights America." PhD diss., University of Oregon, 2017.

Abouguendia, Mona. "Acculturative Stressors, Ethnic Identity, and Psychological Well-Being among Immigrants and Second-Generation Individuals." MEd thesis, University of Alberta, Canada, 2001.

Abo-Zena, Mona M., and Barry, Carolyn M. "Religion and Immigrant-Origin Youth: A Resource and a Challenge." *Research in Human Development* 10.4 (2013) 353–71.

Adekola, Sheri. "Nigerian Women in the Diaspora: The Push and Pull Factors of Migration." MEd thesis, York University, Canada, 2011.

Adewunmi, Oluwatoyin. "Acculturation Stress and the Coping Strategies of Nigerian Immigrant Women in the United States." PhD diss., Walden University, 2015.

Agwu, Chinaka. "Acculturation and Racial Identity Attitudes: An Investigation of First and Second Generation Ibos." MS thesis, Southern Illinois University at Carbondale, 2009.

Ahmed, K. "Adolescent Development for South Asian American Girls." In *Emerging Voices: South Asian Women Redefine Self, Family, and Community*, edited by Gupta S. R., 37–49. New Delhi: Sage, 1999.

Aier, Alivoker. "Re-visiting the Rich Cultural Practices and Values of the Naga Morung in Nagaland: A Proposition for Discipleship in Youth Ministry in Nagaland." *Shalom Journal* 5 (2019).

Ali, Mohamed. "Youth Unemployment." *Harvard International Review* 36.1 (2014) 13–17.

Ali, S. E. A. Mohamed. "The Islam Project: Maps and Islam around the World." *Seasonsali* (blog), October 25, 2011. Online. https://seasonsali.wordpress.com/2011/10/25/the-islam-project-maps-islam-around-the-world.

Arbinger Institute. *The Anatomy of Peace: Resolving the Heart of Conflict*. Oakland: Berrett-Koehler, 2006.

Arbona, Consuelo, et al. "Acculturative Stress Among Documented and Undocumented Latino Immigrants in the United States." *Hispanic Journal of Behavioral Sciences* 32.3 (2010) 362–84.

Archibald, C., and R. Rhodd. "A Measure of Acculturation for Afro-Caribbean Youth." *ABNF* 24.2 (2013) 42–46.

Arthur, John A. *African Diaspora Identities: Negotiating Culture in Transnational Migration*. Lanham, MD: Lexington, 2010

Asante, Godfried Agyeman. "Becoming 'Black' in America: Exploring Racial Identity Development of African Immigrants." MA thesis, Minnesota State University, Mankato, 2012.

Awokoya, Janet Tolulope. "'I'm Not Enough of Anything!': The Racial and Ethnic Identity Constructions and Negotiations of One-Point-Five and Second Generation Nigerians." PhD diss., University of Maryland, College Park, 2009.

Bacio, Guadalupe A., et al. "Drinking Initiation and Problematic Drinking Among Latino Adolescents: Explanations of the Immigrant Paradox." *Psychology of Addictive Behaviors* 27.1 (2013) 14–22.

Berry, John W. "Immigration, Acculturation, and Adaptation." *Applied Psychology* 46.1 (1997) 5–34.

Birman, Dina, and Meredith Poff. "Intergenerational Differences in Acculturation." *Encyclopedia on Early Childhood Development*, April 2011. Online. http://www.child-encyclopedia.com/immigration/according-experts/intergenerational-differences-acculturation.

Bridgewater, M. J., and P. M. Buzzanell. "Caribbean Immigrants' Discourses: Cultural, Moral, and Personal Stories About Workplace Communication in the United States." *Journal of Business Communication* 47.3 (2010) 235–65.

Bowlby, J. "Disruption of Affectional Bonds and Its Effects on Behavior." *Journal of Contemporary Psychotherapy* 2.2 (1970) 75–86.

———. "Processes of Mourning." *International Journal of Psychoanalysis* 42 (1961) 317–40.

Burton, James. "The Most Spoken Languages In America." *WorldAtlas*, June 12, 2018. Online. http://www.worldatlas.com/articles/the-most-spoken-languages-in-america.html.

Butterfield, Sherri-Ann Patrice. "Big Tings a Gwaan: Constructions of Racial and Ethnic Identity among Second-Generation West Indian Immigrants." PhD diss., University of Michigan, 2001.

Carmona, Jose L. "US Youth Employment at 16.1 Percent in July." *Caribbean Business* 41.30 (2013) 10.

Carter, Donald Martin. *Navigating the African Diaspora: The Anthropology of Invisibility*. Minneapolis: University of Minnesota Press, 2010

Cespedes, Yolanda M., and Stanley J. Huey Jr. "Depression in Latino Adolescents: A Cultural Discrepancy Perspective." *Cultural Diversity and Ethnic Minority Psychology* 14.2 (2008) 168–72.

Cha, Peter T. "Ethnic Identity Formation and Participation in Immigrant Churches: Second Generation Korean American Experiences." In *Korean American and Their Religions: Pilgrims and Missionaries from a Different Shore*, edited by H. Kwon et al., 152–55. University Park, PA: Pennsylvania State University Press, 2001.

Chang, Janet, et al. "The Importance of Family Factors and Generation Status: Mental Health Service Use among Latino and Asian Americans." *Cultural Diversity and Ethnic Minority Psychology* 19.3 (2013) 236–47.

Cherng, Hua-Yu Sebastian, et al. "Less Socially Engaged? Participation in Friendship and Extracurricular Activities among Racial/Ethnic Minority and Immigrant Adolescents." *Teachers College Record* 116.3 (2014) 1–28.

Choi, Sun. "Why Did Seung-Hui Cho Kill 32 People?" *New Idea* (blog), March 13, 2014. Online. http://newidea.egloos.com/2135507.

Corduan, Winfried. *Neighboring Faiths*. Downers Grove, IL: InterVarsity, 2012.

Corra, M. K., and S. R. Kimuna. "Double Jeopardy? Female African and Caribbean Immigrants in the United States." *Journal of Ethnic & Migration Studies* 35.6 (2009) 1015–35.

Côté J., and C. Levine. *Identity Formation, Agency, and Culture.* Mahwah, NJ: Lawrence Erlbaum Associates, 2002.

Cross, W. E. "The Negro to Black Conversion Experience: Towards a Psychology of Black Liberation." *Black World* 20 (1971) 13–17.

Dalbey, G. "Recovering Rites of Male Passage." In *The Faith Factor in Fatherhood: Renewing the Sacred Vocation of Fathering,* edited by D. E. Eberly, 291–302. New York: Lexington, 1997.

DellaPergola, Sergio. "World Jewish Population, 2017." *American Jewish Year Book* 117 (2017) 297–380. Online. https://www.jewishdatabank.org/content/upload/bjdb/World_Jewish_Population_2017_AJYB_DataBank_Final.pdf

Dillon, Frank R., et al. "Acculturative Stress and Diminishing Family Cohesion among Recent Latino Immigrants." *Journal of Immigrant and Minority Health* 15.3 (2013) 484–91.

Dufoix, Stéphane. *Diasporas.* Berkeley: University of California Press, 2008.

Erikson, E. H. *Childhood and Society.* New York: Norton, 1963.

———. *Identity: Youth and Crisis.* New York: Norton, 1968.

Falicov, C. J. *Latino Families in Therapy: A Guide to Multicultural Practice.* 2nd ed. New York: Guilford, 2014.

Fournillier, J. B., and T. Lewis. "Finding Voice: Two Afro Caribbean Immigrant Members of the Academy Writing 'Home.'" *Studies in Continuing Education* 32.2 (2010) 147–62.

Gil, R. M., and C. I. Vazquez. *The Maria Paradox: How Latinas Can Merge Old World Traditions With New World Self-Esteem.* New York: Berkley, 1996.

Gomez-Jurado, Jua. *Mad Movie: A Profile of Seung-Hui Cho.* Translated by Bengsun Song. Seoul: Kurie, 2009.

Goosby, B., et al. "Ethnic Differences in Family Stress Processes Among African-Americans and Black Caribbeans." *Journal of African American Studies* 16.3 (2012) 406–22.

Gosk, S., et al. "Desperate Journey: Crime and Poverty Drive Honduran Kids to US." *NBC News,* July 7, 2014. Online. http://www.ws.com/storylinc/immigration-border-risis/desperate-journey-crime-poverty-drive-honduran-kids-u-s-n150011.

Greenblatt, Alan. "What's Causing The Latest Immigration Crisis? A Brief Explainer." *National Public Radio (NPR),* July 9, 2014. Online. http://www.npr.org/2014/07/09/329848538/whats-causing-the-latest-immigration-crisis-a-brief-explainer.

Greenman, Emily. "Educational Attitudes, School Peer Context, and the 'Immigrant Paradox' in Education." *Social Science Research* 42.3 (2013) 698–714.

Guy, Talmadge C. "Black Immigrants of the Caribbean: An Invisible and Forgotten Community." *Adult Learning* 13.1 (2001) 18–21.

Hall, Edward T., and Mildred Reed H. *Understanding Cultural Differences: Germans, French, and Americans.* New York: Anchor, 1987.

Han, Jin Soo. "The History of Korean Immigration to the United States." *KCC Alterna-TV News,* 2005. Online. http://www2.hawaii.edu/~sford/alternatv/s05/articles/jin_history.html.

Hoare, Carol. *Erikson on Development in Adulthood: New Insights from the Unpublished Papers.* Oxford: Oxford University Press, 2002.

Hume, Susan E. "Ethnic and National Identities of Africans in the United States." *Geographical Review* 98.4 (2008) 496–512.

Igielnik, Ruth, and Jens Manuel Krogsad. "Where Refugees to the US Come From." *Pew Research Center*, February 3, 2017. Online. https://www.pewresearch.org/fact-tank/2017/02/03/where-refugees-to-the-u-s-come-from.

"Increase of Korean Population." *Dongpo News*, December 4, 2015. Online. http://www.dongponews.net/news/articleView.html?idxno=30517.

"Issues of Adolescence: Korean American Immigrant History." *Hanho Daily News*, November 14, 2013. Online. http://www.hanhodaily.com/news/articleView.html?idxno=37654.

Jackson, J. S., et al. "Age Cohort, Ancestry, and Immigrant Generation Influences in Family Relations and Psychological Well-Being among Black Caribbean Family Members." *Journal of Social Issues* 63.4 (2007) 729–43.

Jackson, J. S., et al. "Use of Mental Health Services and Subjective Satisfaction with Treatment Among Black Caribbean Immigrants: Results From the National Survey of American Life." *American Journal of Public Health* 97.1 (2007) 60–67.

Joseph, N., et al. "Rules of Engagement: Predictors of Black Caribbean Immigrants' Engagement with African American Culture." *Cultural Diversity and Ethnic Minority Psychology* 19.4 (2013) 414–23.

Joy, Donald. *Empower Your Kids to Be Adults.* Nappanee, IN: Evangel, 2000.

Kalmijn, M. "The Socioeconomic Assimilation of Caribbean American Blacks." *Social Forces* 74.3 (1996) 911–30.

Kapenzi, Geoffrey Z. *The Clash of Cultures: Christian Missionaries and the Shona of Rhodesia (Now Zimbabwe).* Washington, DC: University Press of America, 1979.

Keogh, Bryan. "Hundreds of Toddlers Caught Crossing Border Alone as Immigration Crisis Deepens." *Daily Mail*, June 22, 2014. Online. http://www.dailymail.co.uk/news/article-2665029/Hundreds-TODDLERS-try-cross-border-immigration-crisis-deepens.html.

Kim, M., et al. "Mental Health Problems among Korean American Adolescents." *Psychology* 7 (2006) 1872–82. Online. http://dx.doi.org/10.4236 /psych.2016.714172.

Kohut, H. *The Analysis of the Self: A Systematic Approach to the Psychoanalytic Treatment of Narcissistic Personality Disorders.* The Psychoanalytic Study of the Child 4. New York: International Universities Press, 1971.

———. "Forms and Transformations of Narcissism." In vol. 1 of *The Search for the Self: Selected Writings of Heinz Kohut: 1950–1978*, edited by P. H. Ornstein, 427–60. New York: International Universities Press, 1978.

"Korean Population in USA." *Korea Times Chicago*, September 17, 2016. Online. http://chicagokoreatimes.com/09-17-2016-%EB%AF%B8%EA%B5%AD%EB%82%B4-%ED%95%9C%EC%9D%B8-182%EB%A7%8C2213%EB%AA%85.

Krogstad, Jens Manuel. "Mexicans, Dominicans Are More Catholic than Most Other Hispanics." *Pew Research Center*, May 27, 2014. Online. http://www.pewresearch.org/fact-tank/2014/05/27.

Kundu, S., and G. R. Adams. "Identity Formation, Individuality, and Connectedness in East Indian and Non-East Indian Female Canadian Emerging Adults." *Identity: An International Journal of Theory and Research* 5.3 (2005) 247–60.

Kwon, H., et al. *Korean American and Their Religions: Pilgrims and Missionaries from a Different Shore*. University Park, PA: Pennsylvania State University Press, 2001.

LeaderResources. "J2A Training." *LeaderResources*, 2016. Online. https://www.leaderresources.org/J2A-Training_c_44.html.

Lee, J., et al. "Ethnic Religious Status and Identity Formation: A Qualitative Study of Korean American Christian Youth." *The Journal of Youth Ministry* 5.1 (2006) 9–40.

Lee, Jung Yong. *Marginality: The Key to Multicultural Theology*. Minneapolis: Fortress, 1995.

Lega, Leonor, and Sandra Procel. "Acculturation and Generational Differences in the Irrational Beliefs about Traditional Female Roles in Ecuadorian Mothers and Daughters Living in Ecuador and the United States." *Revista Colombiana de Psicologia* 22.1 (2013) 35–40.

Lorick-Wilmot, Yndia. *Creating Black Caribbean Ethnic Identity*. El Paso: LFB Scholarly, 2010.

Lueck, Kerstin, and Machelle Wilson. "Acculturative Stress in Latino Immigrants: The Impact of Social, Socio-Psychological and Migration-Related Factors." *International Journal of Intercultural Relations* 35.2 (2011) 186–95.

Lukes, Marguerite. "Pushouts, Shutouts, and Holdouts: Adult Education Pathways of Latino Young Adults." *Immigration Policy Institute*, September 6, 2012. Online. http://migrationpolicy.org/article/mexican-immigrants-united-states.

Marcia, J. E. "Development and Validation of Ego Identity Status." *Journal of Personality and Social Psychology* 3 (1966) 551–58.

———. "Identity in Adolescence." In *Handbook of Adolescent Psychology*, edited by J. Adelson, 151–72. New York: Wiley, 1980.

Marin, G. S., and R. J. Gamba. "A New Measurement of Acculturation for Hispanics: The Bidimensional Acculturation Scale for Hispanics (BAS)." *Hispanic Journal of Behavioral Sciences* 18.3 (1996) 297–316.

Markham, Ian S., and Christy Lohr. *A World Religions Reader*. West Sussex, UK: Wiley-Blackwell. 2009.

Martin, J. N., and Thomas K. Nakayama. *Intercultural Communication in Contexts*. 5th ed. Boston: McGraw-Hill, 2010.

Martinez, Michael, and Hurtado, Jaqueline. "Central American Immigrant Parents Agonize When Child Crosses Border Alone." *CNN*, June 22, 2014. Online. http://www.cnn.com/2014/06/21/us/central-american-family-agony-child-border-crossings.

Mather, Mark. "Children in US Immigrant Families Chart New Path." *Population Reference Bureau*, March 24, 2009. Online. https://www.prb.org/childreninimmigrantfamilies.

Maticka-Tyndale, E., et al. "A Profile of the Sexual Experiences of African, Caribbean, and Black Canadian Youth in the Context of Canadian Youth Sexuality." *Canadian Journal of Human Sexuality* 25.1 (2016) 41–52.

Mbiti, J. *African Religions and Philosophies*. 2nd ed. Portsmouth, NH: Heinemann, 1997.

———. *Introduction to African Religions*. 2nd ed. Oxford: Heinemann International, 1991.

"Mexican Immigrants in the United States, 2008." *Pew Research Center*, April 15, 2009. Online. https://www.pewresearch.org/hispanic/2009/04/15/mexican-immigrants-in-the-united-states-2008.

Min, P. G. "The Attachments of New York City Caribbean Indian Immigrants to Indian Culture, Indian Immigrants, and India." *Journal of Ethnic & Migration Studies* 39.10 (2013) 1601–1616.

Model, S. *West Indian Immigrants: A Black Success Story?* New York: Russell Sage Foundation, 2011.

Model, S., et al. "Black Caribbeans in Comparative Perspective." *Journal of Ethnic & Migration Studies* 25.2 (1999) 187.

Mucherera, Tapiwa N. *Counseling and Pastoral Care in African and Other Cross-Cultural Contexts.* Eugene, OR: Wipf & Stock, 2017.

———. *Meet Me at the Palaver: Narrative Pastoral Counseling in Postcolonial Contexts.* Eugene, OR: Cascade, 2009.

Murphy, E. J., and R. Mahalingam. "Perceived Congruence between Expectations and Outcomes: Implications for Mental Health among Caribbean Immigrants." *American Journal of Orthopsychiatry* 76.1 (2006) 120–27.

Murray, Henry A., and Clyde Kluckhohn. *Personality in Nature, Society, and Culture.* New York: Knopf, 1953.

Nathan, R. A. "Black Theology in Britain." *A Journal of Contextual Praxis* 1 (1998) 1–16.

———. "African-Caribbean Youth Identity in the United Kingdom." *International Review of Mission* 89.354 (2000) 349.

National Center for Education Statistics (NCES). "Education Longitudinal Study of 2002." Institute of Education Sciences, US Department of Education. Online. https://nces.ed.gov/surveys/els2002.

Nazario, Sonia. *Enrique's Journey.* New York: Random House, 2006.

Nouwen, H. *The Return of the Prodigal Son: A Story of Homecoming.* New York: Doubleday, 1992.

Nwoji, Stanley. "The Missional Status of African Christians in Diaspora: A Case of the African Christian Fellowship and African-Led Churches in the United States of America." PhD diss., Asbury Theological Seminary, 2009.

Nzegwu, Nkiru, and Isidore Okpewho. *The New African Diaspora.* Bloomington: Indiana University Press, 2009.

Odera, Lilian A. "Acculturation, Coping Styles, and Mental Health of First-Generation Kenyan Immigrants in the United States." PhD diss., University of Michigan, 2007.

Oduyoye, Mercy A. "The Value of African Religious Beliefs and Practices for Christian Theology." In *African Theology En Route*, edited by K. Appiah-Kubi and S. Torres, 100–101. Maryknoll, NY: Orbis, 1979.

Ombaba, Renee N. "In a Foreign Land: Stories of African Immigrants and Their Children in Jackson, MS." MA thesis, University of Mississippi, 2014.

Orozco, C., and J. Rhodes. "Unraveling the Immigrant Paradox, Youth & Society." 20.10 (2009) 1–33.

Pearce, L. D., and M. L. Denton. *A Faith of Their Own: Stability and Change in the Religiosiy of America's Adolescents.* Oxford: Oxford University Press, 2011.

Phinney, J. "Stages of Ethnic Identity Development in Minority Group Adolescents." *Journal of Early Adolescence* 9 (1993) 34–49.

Pocock, Michael. *Diaspora Missiology: Reflections on Reaching the Scattered Peoples of the World.* Evangelical Missiological Society Series 23. Pasadena, CA: William Carey, 2015.

Portes, Alejandro, and Rubén G. Rumbaut. *Children of Immigrants Longitudinal Study (CILS), 1991–2006 (ICPSR 20520)*. Ann Arbor, MI: Inter-University Consortium for Political and Social Research, 2012. Online. http://doi.org/10.3886/ICPSR20520.v2.

Portillo Villeda, Suyapa, and Gerardo Torres Zelaya. "Why Are Honduran Children Leaving?" *Counter Punch*, June 27, 2014. Online. http://www.counterpunch.org/2014/06/27/why-are-honduran-children-leaving.

Prah, Pamela M. "Number of Undocumented Children Who Cross US Border Alone Has Tripled." *Stateline*, May 9, 2013. Online. https://www.pewtrusts.org/en/research-and-analysis/blogs/stateline/2013/05/09/number-of-undocumented-children-who-cross-us-border-alone-has-tripled.

Ramirez, Margaret. "New Islamic Movement Seeks Latino Converts." *LA Times*, March 15, 1999. Online. https://www.latimes.com/archives/la-xpm-1999-mar-15-me-17467-story.html.

Ramirez, Rosa. "More Central American Kids Crossing Solo." *National Journal*, December 7, 2012. Online. http://www.nationaljournal.com/thenextamerica/immigration/more-central-america-kids-crossing-solo-20120807.

Redlener, Irwin. "Undocumented Children Need Charitable Help." *USA Today*, June 25, 2014. Online. http://www.usatoday.com/story/opinion/2014/06/25/immigration-

Regis, H. A. "A Theoretical Framework for the Investigation of the Role and Significance of Communication in the Development of the Sense of Community among English-Speaking Caribbean Immigrants." *Howard Journal of Communications* 2.1 (1989) 57–80.

Rhodes, R. L., et al. *Assessing Culturally and Linguistically Diverse Students: A Practical Guide*. New York: Guilford. 2005.

Roopnarine, J. L., et al. "Beliefs about Mothers' and Fathers' Roles and the Division of Child Care and Household Labor in Indo-Caribbean Immigrants with Young Children." *Cultural Diversity and Ethnic Minority Psychology* 15.2 (2009) 173–82.

Rotheram, M. J., and J. Phinney. "Introduction: Definitions and Perspectives in the Study of Children's Ethnic Socialization." In *Children's Ethnic Socialization*, edited by J. S. Phinney and M. J. Rotheram, 10–28. Newbury Park, CA: Sage, 1987.

Ruggiero, K. *The Jewish Diaspora in Latin America and the Caribbean: Fragments of Memory*. Sussex: Sussex Academic, 2005.

Rumbaut, Ruben G. "The Crucible Within: Ethnic Identity, Self-Esteem, and Segmented Assimilation among Children of Immigrants." *International Migration Review* 28.4 (1994) 748–94.

———. "Reaping What You Sew: Immigration, Youth, and Reactive Ethnicity." *Applied Developmental Science* 22.2 (2008) 1–4.

———. "Sites of Belonging: Acculturation, Discrimination, and Ethnic Identity Among Children of Immigrants." In *Discovering Successful Pathways in Children's Development: Mixed Methods in the Study of Childhood and Family Life*, edited by Thomas S. Weisner, 111–62. Chicago: University of Chicago Press, 2005.

Ryan, Camille. "Language Use in the United States: 2011." American Community Survey Reports. *US Census Bureau*, August 6, 2013. Online. https://www2.census.gov/library/publications/2013/acs/acs-22/acs-22.pdf.

Rynkiewich, Michael A. "Pacific Islands Diaspora Studies." *Pacific Studies* 35.1/2 (2012).

Safransky, Sy. "Psychotherapy." *Yoga Journal*, May/June 1992. 52–53.

Sanchez, D. "Racial and Ego Identity Development in Black Caribbean College Students." *Journal of Diversity in Higher Education* 6.2 (2013) 115–26.

Scott, Laurel E. "To Welcome the Stranger: Hospitality with Ghanaian Immigrants in the United Methodist Church." PhD diss., Boston University, 2014.

Seaton, Eleanor K., et al. "An Intersectional Approach for Understanding Perceived Discrimination and Psychological Well-Being Among African American and Caribbean Black Youth." *Developmental Psychology* 46.5 (2010) 1372–79.

Seaton, Eleanor K., et al. "The Prevalence of Perceived Discrimination among African American and Caribbean Black Youth." *Developmental Psychology* 44.5 (2008) 1288–97.

Shervin, Assari, and Cleopatra Howard Caldwell. "Neighborhood Safety and Major Depressive Disorder in a National Sample of Black Youth; Gender by Ethnic Differences." *Children (Basel)* 4.2 (2017) 14–28.

Smith, A., et al. "Serial Migration and Its Implications for the Parent-Child Relationship: A Retrospective Analysis of the Experiences of the Children of Caribbean Immigrants." *Cultural Diversity and Ethnic Minority Psychology* 10.2 (2004) 107–22.

St. Louis, G. M., and J. H. Liem. "Ego Identity, Ethnic Identity, and the Psychosocial Well Being of Ethnic Minority and Majority College Students." *Identity: An International Journal of Theory and Research* 5.3 (2005) 227–46.

Stoney, Sierra, and Jeanne Batalova. "Mexican Immigrants in the United States." *Immigration Policy Institute*, February 28, 2013. Online. http://migrationpolicy.org/article/mexican-immigrants-united-states.

Stoney, Sierra, et al. "South American Immigrants in the United States." *Migration Policy Institute*, May 2, 2013. Online. http://www.migrationpolicy.org/article/south-american-immigrants-united-states.

Strama, Inez. "Deconstructing the American Dream: Exploring Ethnic Identity and Subjective Social Status in 1.5-Generation Immigrants." PsyD diss., Massachusetts School of Professional Psychology, 2015.

Suárez-Orozco, Carola, and J. Rhodes. "Unraveling the Immigrant Paradox." *Youth & Society* 20.10 (2009) 1–33.

Suárez-Orozco, Carola, and Marcelo Suárez-Orozco. *Transformations: Migration, Family Life, and Achievement Motivation among Latino Adolescents*. Stanford, CA: Stanford University Press, 1995.

Sue, Derlad Wing, and Sue David. *Counseling the Culturally Diverse*. 5th ed. New Jersey: Wiley & Sons, 2013.

Taylor, R., et al. "Comorbid Mood and Anxiety Disorders, Suicidal Behavior, and Substance Abuse among Black Caribbeans in the USA." *Journal of African American Studies* 17.4 (2013) 409–25.

Thobaben, James. "Pilgrimage in the Christian Life." Chapel address delivered November 18, 2016. Video. Online. https://vimeo.com/192170571.

Thomas, K. J. A. "Socio-Demographic Determinants of Language Transition among the Children of French- and Spanish-Caribbean Immigrants in the US." *Journal of Ethnic & Migration Studies* 37.4 (2011) 543–59.

Tira, S. T., and T. Yamamori, eds. *Scattered and Gathered: A Global Compendium of Diaspora Missiology*. Regnum Books International. Eugene, OR: Wipf & Stock, 2016.

Turner, Victor W. *The Ritual Process: Structure and Anti-Structure*. The Lewis Henry Morgan Lectures. Chicago: Aldine, 1969.

"*Under the Same Moon* (2007) Plot." *IMDb*. Online. http://www.imdb.com/title/tt0796307/plotsummary.

United States Census Bureau. "2012 ACS 1-year Estimates." *American Community Survey,* June 7, 2019. Online. https://www.census.gov/programs-surveys/acs/technical-documentation/table-and-geography-changes/2012/1-year.html.

United States Department of Homeland Security (USDHS). *2008 Yearbook of Immigration Statistics.* Washington, DC: Office of Immigration Statistics, 2009. Online. https://www.dhs.gov/xlibrary/assets/statistics/yearbook/2008/ois_yb_2008.pdf.

Van Gennep, A. "*Les rites de passage* (in French). Paris: Émile Nourry. Lay Summary—Review by Frederick Starr." *The American Journal of Sociology* 15.5 (1909) 707–9.

Vazquez, C. I., and D. Rosa. *Grief Therapy with Latinos: Integrating Culture for Clinicians.* New York: Springer, 2011.

"Virginia Tech Shootings Fast Facts." *CNN,* April 3, 2017. Online. http://www.cnn.com/2013/10/31/us/virginia-tech-shootings-fast-facts/index.html.

Warner, Gregory. "How One Kenyan Tribe Produces the World's Best Runners." *National Public Radio (NPR),* November 1, 2013. Online. https://www.npr.org/sections/parallels/2013/11/01/241895965/how-one-kenyan-tribe-produces-the-worlds-best-runners.

Wheeler, D. P., and A. M. Mahoney. "Caribbean Immigrants in the United States—Health and Health Care: The Need for a Social Agenda." *Health & Social Work* 33.3 (2008) 238–40.

Williams, D. R., et al. "The Mental Health of Black Caribbean Immigrants: Results from the National Survey of American Life." *American Journal of Public Health* 97.1 (2007) 52–59.

Wilson, E. S. "What It Means to Become a United States American: Afro-Caribbean Immigrants' Constructions of American Citizenship and Experience of Cultural Transition." *Journal of Ethnographic & Qualitative Research* 3.3 (2009) 196–204.

Winnicott, D. "Transitional Objects and Transitional Phenomena." *The International Journal of Psychoanalysis* 35 (1953).

Yu, Jundhee. "Fun & Easy Guide: Korean Confucian Ideals." December 23, 2015. Online. http://kid.chosun.com/site/data/html_dir/2015/12/23/2015122302276.html.

Zahniser, A. H., and D. L. Whiteman. *Symbol and Ceremony: Making Disciples Across Cultures.* Monrovia, CA: MARC, 1997.

Zong, Jie, and Jeanne Batalova. "South American Immigrants in the United States." *Migration Policy Institute,* November 7, 2018. Online. https://www.migrationpolicy.org/article/south-american-immigrants-united-states.

Contributors

Janet Diaz is the Director of Evangelization at the multicultural parish Church of the Holy Family in Novi, Michigan. Prior to her current role, she served as the Dean of the Institute for Ministry at Sacred Heart Major Seminary in Detroit, overseeing the formation of lay students of diverse cultural backgrounds. Before working at the seminary, Dr. Diaz served in several lay ministry roles, with an emphasis on ministry with Hispanics. She earned her Master of Arts in Pastoral Studies at Sacred Heart and her Doctor of Ministry at Barry University.

Anthony (Tony) Headley is professor of counseling at Asbury Theological Seminary, where he has served since 1990. He is an ordained elder in the Free Methodist Church-USA and a licensed psychologist and Health Service Provider in Kentucky. He also holds an MDiv from Asbury Theological Seminary. From the University of Kentucky, he holds a PhD in counseling psychology as well as master's degrees in family studies and counseling psychology. He also holds a BA in Christian ministries from Ohio Christian University.

Dr. Headley has authored five books: *Achieving Balance in Ministry* (1999); *Created for Responsibility* (2006; 2015); *Reframing Your Ministry* (2007); *Family Crucible: The Influence of Family Dynamics in the Life and Ministry of John Wesley* (2010); and *Getting It Right: Christian Perfection and Wesley's Purposeful List* (2013). In addition, he has authored book chapters and articles in various publications. He frequently conducts training and development seminars for church and clergy groups on topics such as stress management, burnout, self-care, conflict resolution and boundaries across the USA and overseas. He is married to Adina, who is a minister in her own right, conducting retreats with various women's group in the US and internationally. He has three adult sons.

Sam Kim received a PhD from Asbury Theological seminary (Intercultural Studies). She is an ordained pastor and an assistant professor at the E. Stanley Jones School of World Mission at Asbury Theological Seminary. Sam was a missionary in the Middle East for fifteen years before coming to Asbury. She has written several books and articles, including *Identity Crisis: Standing between Two Identities of Women Believers from Muslim Backgrounds in Jordan* (2015).

Mercy Langat is a PhD candidate in the Intercultural Studies program at Asbury Theological Seminary. Her research focus is on Diaspora Missiology with particular interests in immigration, race, ethnicity as well as liminal and hybrid identity formation among immigrant women.

Dinelia Rosa, PhD, Licensed Psychologist, is director of the Dean-Hope Center for Educational and Psychological services at Teachers College (TC). She coordinates the practicum for students at five graduate programs and teaches and supervises Clinical Psychology program at TC. She is a founding member of several initiatives including: the TC psychological emergency Response Team (PERT) and supervises the Clinical Graduate student serving on this team; the Health Psychology rotation in the Bellevue-NYU internship Program; and the Division of Culture Race and Ethnicity at the New York State Psychological Association (NYPSA). Dr. Rosa is interested in research associated with treatment outcome measures and has led research initiatives at Dean Hope Center. In addition, she is interested in issues of bilingualism in training and has received the APA Committee of Ethnic Minority Recruitment, Retention and Training (CEMRRAT) grant to address needs of graduate student in clinical and counseling psychology.

About the Editors

Anne Kiome Gatobu, PhD, is former Dean of the School of Practical Theology and Associate Professor of Pastoral Care & Counseling, Asbury Theology Seminary. Gatobu is experienced as a pastoral psychotherapist in trauma and family counseling. She is an Ordained Elder with United Methodist Church and is currently serving as the District Superintendent for Kansas City District of the Great Plains Annual Conference. She received her BA from the University of Nairobi (1990); an MA in pastoral care and counseling from Iliff School of Theology (1997); a PhD from the University of Denver and Iliff School of Theology (2006); and an MDiv from Iliff School of Theology (2008).

Gatobu's scholarship is in religious and psychological studies. Her research interests revolve around issues of integration between Christian faith, psychology, and social-cultural contextualization with specific focus on Clergy Health ministries, gender violence, immigrant families, and cross-cultural issues. Born and raised in Kenya, Gatobu's contribution to the academy and ministry is always augmented with a global worldview. She is the author of *Female Identity Formation and Response to Intimate Trauma: A Case Study of Domestic Violence in Kenya*. She has also authored several articles and chapters in books.

She is the founder of *FOWCUS-Kenya*—a nonprofit, US-based ministry to orphaned children and women in Kenya—and has organized mission trips to Africa since 2004. She is also the founder of *Flourishing Springs*, an initiative that offers coaching and training on selfcare, and intervention with conflicted churches.

Chris Kiesling, PhD, has served as Professor of Human Development and Christian Discipleship at Asbury Theological Seminary for over two decades. During his tenure at Asbury, he served four years as Interim Dean of the School of Practical Theology. He holds a Master of Divinity degree from Asbury Theological seminary and a Doctoral degree from Texas Tech University, where he focused his dissertation on spiritual identity formation. He is an ordained Elder of the United Methodist Church, Northwest Texas Annual Conference. Prior to the professorate, he served as pastor of Manchester UMC in rural Arkansas, campus ministry director at Henderson State University where he also served as Adjunct professor teaching Humanities, campus ministry director at Ouachita Baptist University, and as Associate Pastor at First UMC in Lubbock, Texas. He is the co-author of *Spiritual Formation in Emerging Adulthood* (2013), and has written numerous other chapters, articles, and editorial pieces for scholarly and popular publications.

Tapiwa N. Mucherera, PhD, Professor of Pastoral Care and Counseling at Asbury Theological Seminary, an ordained Elder of United Methodist Church, and a member in full connection with the Zimbabwe West Annual Conference. He is also an Affiliated Member of the Florida United Methodist Annual conference and serves on the Board of Ordained Ministry. He served on the ACPE National Board as a National Seminary Representative for eight years. He has served several churches in Zimbabwe, Chicago, Iowa, Denver, and Kentucky. He is author of four books: *Glimmers of Hope* (2013); *Meet Me at the Palaver* (2009); *Pastoral Care from a Third World Perspective* (2001, 2005); and *Counseling and Pastoral Care in African and Other Cross-Cultural Contexts* (2017). He has chapters in Anne E. Streaty Wimberly, *Keep It Real: Working with Today's Black Youth* (2005), and Stephen Madigen, *Therapy from Outside In* (2004). He was co-editor (with Emmanuel Lartey) on the recently published *Pastoral Care, Health, Healing, and Wholeness in African Contexts* (2017).